# Roots
## *of the*
# Reformation

### *By Karl Adam*

Translated by Cecily Hastings

*A Coming Home* Resource

This edition of Karl Adam's *Roots of the Reformation* is dedicated to men and woman who have placed their faith in Jesus Christ and dedicated their own lives to the service of truth at whatever cost, following in the footsteps of such great Christian witnesses as Barnabas the Apostle, Edmund Campion, Issac Jogues, and Francis de Sales.

# Roots
*of the*
# Reformation

*By Karl Adam*

Translated by Cecily Hastings

*A Coming Home* Resource

Published by
Coming Home Resources
an imprint of
The Coming Home Network International
Scarpone Professional Building
2021 Sunset Blvd., Suite 2
Steubenville, Ohio 43952
(800) 664-5110

Cover design and layout by
Beth Hart

Published in the United States of America
ISBN 0-9702621-0-8

# Contents

# Author's Foreword

The following lectures[Ψ] were delivered in 1947 to a large gathering of the *Una Sancta* movement at Stuttgart and Karlsruhe. The ideas here advanced are often closely related to those expressed by Johannes Hessen in his stimulating work, *Luther in Katholischer Sicht* (Bonn, 1947). I did not actually see his book until after I had given my lectures. Hessen gives a philosophical and historical account of the "phenomenon of Luther" and the possibility of an ultimate understanding with the Lutheran Church. It is my aim to provide this with a clear theological basis.

It cannot be doubted that at the present moment, under the shattering impact of two world wars, a bridge is being built between Catholics and Lutherans, at least in the sense that the unreality of mere polemic is being abandoned, that Luther on the one hand and the Papacy on the other are being seen in a clearer and more friendly light, and that real efforts are being made, by Christians everywhere, to bring about if not a *unio fidei* [union of faith] at least a *unio caritatis* [union of heart].

Since Luther can only be understood against the background of the ecclesiastical abuses of the late Middle Ages, I could not avoid dealing with these abuses in detail. I have deliberately taken my evidence exclusively from Catholic sources, especially from Karl Bihlmeyer's history of the Church (the objectivity and thoroughness of which have made it the standard work on the subject), and Josef Lortz's brilliant and

---

Ψ This book is a large part of *One and Holy*, a translation of *Una Sancta in Katholischer Sicht*, published by Patmos Verlag, Dusseldorf, Germany.

psychologically penetrating *Reformation in Deutschland*. In the light of recent researches it should hardly be necessary to emphasize that these abuses do not give the whole picture of the medieval Church. Its darker aspects are relieved by so many bright lights that it is not possible to take a pessimistic view of it as a whole.

KARL ADAM
1951

# Introduction

One way to understand the thousands of different and divergent Christian denominations that have emerged from the Reformation of the sixteenth century is as a large tree supporting a multitude of branches, each branch representing a different faith tradition in their witness to Jesus Christ. There are many opinions as to what this tree means or represents, but if we go deeper into this metaphor and move beyond what is commonly seen to what is generally hidden—to the "roots" that gave birth to that tree—we confront some very important and challenging questions: What actually led to the decisions by not one but by many to divide a fifteen hundred year old unified though suffering Church into, initially, dozens of fragments? Why did this happen, and what does this continued fragmentation mean? Should it continue to exist, and how can *I* reconcile these issues today?

Too often books on the Reformation are unapologetically polemical, biased to one side or the other. But Professor Karl Adam is painfully objective in his examination of the issues and the people that shaped the Reformation. And as a Catholic theologian and historian, he does not exempt from criticism even Rome itself.

In 1947, Karl Adam gave a series of lectures on this subject which were later compiled into his 1951 book, *One and Holy*, published originally in Germany by Patmos Verlag in Dusseldorf. Because it was so well received by Catholics and Protestants alike, it was then translated into English by Cecily Hastings and published by Sheed & Ward in New York. Five years later Sheed & Ward published *The Roots of the*

*Reformation*, an edited and smaller version of *One and Holy*. Recognizing that this out-of-print book has far from out-lived its usefulness, the *Coming Home Network* decided to reprint it, adding extensive biographical and historical endnotes to make it more accessible and useful to the modern reader. The result is the current edition now in your hands. For your convenience the following format has been implemented:

The symbol 'Ψ' represents Karl Adam's original footnotes, which are found at the bottom of the page on which it appears.

The asterisk '\*' follows the names of persons for whom a paragraph of information can be found in Appendix A (historical figures). A page number within parenthesis (p.1) appears at the end of each biographical paragraph, referring the reader back to the page on which the person's name was mentioned.

A superscript number ([1,2,3...etc]) following various historical references made in the text directs the reader to Appendix B (historical footnotes) where further explanation or clarification can be found.

All text within brackets [ ] was inserted by the *CHNetwork*, to explain, for example, the meaning of Latin terms.

*Coming Home Resources* (an imprint of *The Coming Home Network International*) has published this edition of *The Roots of the Reformation* in hope and prayer that it will be helpful and informative for both our Protestant and Catholic readers.

Chris Erickson
Director, *The Coming Home Network*

# CHAPTER ONE

# Weakness in the Church

## Avarice in Rome

Modern historians are agreed that the roots of the Reformation reach far back into the high Middle Ages. The former monk of Cluny, Pope Gregory VII [1073-1085], in his zeal for the liberty and reform of the Church, so interpreted the papal claims formulated by Augustine,* Pope Gregory the Great [Gregory I, 540-604] and Pope Nicholas I [858-867] that right up into the late Middle Ages they excited repeated resistance from the secular powers, shook the prestige of the Papal See and so prepared the way for Luther's Reformation. Gregory's *Dictatus Papae*,[1] in which he claimed for the Pope a direct authority even over secular affairs, with the right to depose unworthy princes and release their subjects from their oath of allegiance, inspired papal policy all through the Middle Ages.

This certainly added a corrosive bitterness and a devastating violence—a violence which did not stop short of the Papal See itself—to the conflicts which in any event would have been bitter enough between *Regnum* [rule] and *Sacerdotium*[2] [sacred], the struggle between the Emperor Henry IV [1050-1108] and the Pope over investitures,[3] the battles with the Hohenstaufen,[4] Frederick Barbarossa* and Frederick II,* the conflicts with Philip the Fair* of France and Ludwig of Bavaria. In Frederick II's Manifesto of 1230 Pope Gregory IX [1227-1241] is already branded as "the great Dragon and Antichrist of the last days." In 1301 Philip the Fair had Pope Boniface VIII's [1294-1303] Bull[5]*Ausculta*[6] publicly burned, and in 1303 had the Pope himself taken into custody as a "heretic, blasphemer and simoniac."

Ludwig of Bavaria, supported by the Franciscan Spirituals,[7] declared Pope John XXII [1316-1334] a "formal heretic" in the Reichstag[8] at Nuremberg in 1323.

The counter-attack of the "spiritual sword" was a series of excommunications,[9] extending to the fourth degree of kindred, and years of interdict[10] over whole countries. Germany alone was under interdict for twenty years, which meant that no public religious service could be held, no sacrament could be publicly administered, no bell could sound. The more often these ecclesiastical penalties were imposed, the blunter grew the spiritual sword. Inevitably the religion and morality of the people suffered serious damage, their sense of the Church was weakened, their sympathies were alienated from Christ's vicar.[11] In due course there arose theologians amongst the Franciscan Spirituals, particularly their General Michael of Cesena,* and William of Ockham,* who in numerous writings questioned the founding by Christ of the Papacy as the Church knows it. And Marsilius of Padua* in 1324 drew up a revolutionary programme entitled *Defensor Pacis*,[12] with a theory of Church and State which broke completely with existing ecclesiastical constitutions—"a significant prelude to the Reformation."

Anti-papal feeling in Germany gained ground when, in 1314, the See of Rome moved to Avignon[13] and was thus brought completely under French influence, and again when the financial burdens arising out of the double establishment at Rome and Avignon compelled the Pope to build up a system of taxation which, when expanded, weighed heavily both on spiritual and on economic life. The Camera Apostolica[14] covered the whole Church with a net of taxation called the Census. Besides the revenues of the Papal State, this included pallium-money (the tax paid by newly appointed archbishops, bishops and abbots), *spolia* (the total assets of deceased prelates), the numerous administrative taxes and procurations for papal visitations; above all, the taxes on the revenues of vacant benefices, and annates (payment of the first year's income, or at least half of it, from all ecclesiastical appointments made by the pope). Since Pope Clement IV [1265-1268] had claimed for the Pope unlimited authority over all ecclesiastical appointments in Christendom, the number of benefices reserved to the Pope had risen beyond computation. This aroused general opposition, especially when John XXII in the course of his conflict with Lugwig of Bavaria, tried to fill all the vacant sees and offices in Germany with his own supporters.

## Benefices & Taxation

In a similar spirit, but contrary to prevailing ecclesiastical law, the Papal Chancellery in the fourteenth and fifteenth centuries encouraged *cumulus beneficiorum* i.e., the holding of many benefices by one person, and commendation, by which a benefice could be conferred simply for the income derived from it, without the holder's having any spiritual obligations to fulfil. Moreover, the Pope could promise to provide a person to a benefice even before its present occupant had actually died.

The spirit of mammon had won such an ascendancy in the Curia[15] that Pope Clement VII [1523-1534], for example, at the very height of the Reformation storm, was trying to make money from the sale of Cardinals' hats. It is against this background that we must understand the denunciation of the great Catholic preacher Geiler von Kaisersberg:* "It is no longer the Holy Ghost who appoints the rulers of the Church, but the devil, and for money, for favor and by bribery of the Cardinals."Ψ

It is easily understandable that the Curia's irresponsible policies in matters of taxation and appointments, together with the

---

Ψ A less severe judgement on this matter is given by Barraclough, *Papal Provisions.* (Trans.)

arbitrary occupation of ecclesiastical offices in Germany by foreigners, gravely limited orderly diocesan government, and that they aroused on all sides uncertainty in regard to the law and consequent discontent amounting to unrest and resistance. There were expensive lawsuits that had to be taken to the highest papal court, the Roman Rota.[16] The German nation had its public grievances (*gravamina nationis Germanicae*). They were raised for the first time in 1456 by Archbishop Dietrich of Mainz at the Fürstentag at Frankfurt. From then on they came up again and again in the Reichstag in the form in which the humanist Jakob Wimpfiling* had consolidated them. But the abuses, so far from being removed, mounted from year to year as the papal requirements increased.

The Pope's yearly income was greater than that of any German Emperor. John XXII, for instance, died leaving three-quarters of a million gold coins in his treasury: a figure so high, considering the values and conditions of the time, that it was bound to have a catastrophic effect on the believer when he pictured against this background the poor tent-maker Paul, or the still poorer fisherman Peter, coming with dusty sandals to Rome and bringing nothing with them but a deep and noble desire to preach Christ and to die for Christ.

### The Great Schism

If the fiscal policy of Avignon, where the Popes had their court for sixty-five years, seriously damaged the political and economic interests of German Christianity and so at least indirectly undermined the religious authority of the Pope, the great Schism of the West,[17] from 1378 to 1417, threatened the prestige of the Papacy with final extinction.

In opposition to Pope Urban VI,* elected under pressure from the Roman people and disliked for various reasons, the French Cardinals in Avignon, the so-called "ultramontani,"[18] declaring the election unfree and invalid, raised a cousin of the

French King to the papal chair as Clement VII, and Christendom was split into two camps. The division went right through the Christian body. Whole Orders, such as the Cistercians, Carthusians, Franciscans, Dominicans and Carmelites, fell into two halves. And since both Popes excommunicated each other and each other's supporters, the whole of Christendom was at least nominally excommunicate.

The split did not come to an end with the deaths of the two Popes, for the Cardinals in Rome and Avignon all obstinately held their own papal elections. Matters grew worse when the Council of Pisa,[19] in 1409, deposed both the Rome and Avignon Popes as "notorious schismatics and heretics" and elected a third, Alexander V, who soon died, and was followed by John XXIII. Since both the deposed Popes obstinately maintained the validity of their elections this led, not to unity, but "from wicked duality to accursed triplicity." It was only in 1417, with the election of Martin V at the Council of Constance,[20] that the Church could acknowledge one single head again in place of the three previously elected claimants.

It was inevitable that this schism of nearly forty years should shake the Church to her foundation; that radicals of the type of William of Ockham and Marsilius of Padua should formulate a democratic theory of the Church, taking the plenitude of ecclesiastical authority to rest in the body of the faithful, not in a single head; that thoughtful theologians such as Peter d'Ailly and the distinguished John Gerson should construct the so-called conciliar theory, making the Pope subordinate to a General Council and giving the Church a parliamentary instead of a monarchical constitution. The idea of the Church received from the Fathers—in which there was but *one* Rock, *one* Keeper of the Keys, *one* Shepherd—began to weaken. Trust in the Father of Christendom was gone. In this sense, the experience of the Great Schism had impressed its decisive stamp on the minds of the faithful (Lortz).

## Moral Collapse

Hard upon the dogmatic attack on papal authority inevitably conjured up by the Great Western Schism, there followed its moral collapse; the Renaissance Popes seem to have carried out in their own lives that worship of idolatrous humanism, demonic ambition and unrestrained sensuality which was in many ways bound up with the reawakening of the ancient ideal of manhood. The most sober ecclesiastical historians agree that the reigns of the Popes from Sixtus IV [1471-1484] to Leo X [1513-1521] "represent, from the religious and ecclesiastical point of view, the lowest level of the Papacy since the tenth and eleventh centuries" (Bihlmeyer, vol. ii, p. 477).

The unbridled nepotism[21] of Sixtus IV, which threatened to degrade the Papacy to "a dynastic heritage and the *Patrimonium Petri* [heritage of Peter] to a petty Italian state" (Lortz, vol. i. p. 75), was followed by the fateful Bull against witches[22] issued by Pope Innocent VIII [1484-1492], a man of scandalous life. Worse still was the conduct of Pope Alexander VI* [1492-1503], stained with murder and impurity, and the demonic lust for blood and power of his son Cesare Borgia. Then came the burning of the Dominican Savonarola at Alexander's orders, the sheer political jugglery of Pope Julius II [1503-1513], whose pontificate was dissipated in campaigns and wars, and finally the pleasure-loving worldliness of Pope Leo X [1513-1521], who found the chase and the theatre more important than Martin Luther and his religious aspirations.

The reputation of the Papacy was dragged not merely in the dust but in the mud. It is especially significant of the mentality of Leo X and of the Renaissance Popes in general, that in the solemn procession at his enthronement in the papal chair, the Most Blessed Sacrament was accompanied by statues of naked pagan gods, with the inscription "First Venus reigned [the age of Alexander VI], then Mars [in the time of

Julius II], and now [under Leo X] Pallas Athene holds the scepter" (Lortz, vol. i, p. 86).

The news of these scandalous doings, of course, soon crossed the Alps and stripped the last vestige of credit from the Mother of Christendom. The humanist circles at Erfurt and Florence took care of that, and so later did Ulrich von Hutten* and the Dunkelmänner letters. Nor was Luther himself far behind them. Even when he was translating the Bible in 1522, before he had reached the hey-day of his hatred for Rome, he depicted the great Harlot of the Apocalypse as wearing the triple papal crown.

## Darkness in Germany

Let us turn now from the crying scandals surrounding the highest ecclesiastical authority to the abuses which marred the German Church and her spiritual life before Luther's advent.

It is certainly not true to say that the German Church which witnessed these scandals in the Roman government was herself ripe for destruction. The constant urge for reform and the tremendous response when Luther raised the alarm would be incomprehensible if Christian life had died out completely. We can even assert that German Christianity in the last phase of the Middle Ages was, in spite of all, more devout than it is today. For today a denunciation of abuses by a Martin Luther would cause no revolution. It was the age of the three Catherines, of Siena, Bologna and Genoa;[23] the age when St. Bridget* scourged the abuses of the Avignon Curia with the flames of her wrath, when Thomas à Kempis [1379-1471] wrote his immortal *Imitation of Christ*, when an unknown priest wrote the *Theologia Germanica*[24] first published by Luther. It was the age in which German mysticism flowered in Eckhardt, Tauler and Suso, and the *devotio moderna*[25] of the "Brothers of the Common Life" was aspiring to revivify, spiritualize and personalize benumbed Christianity.

The evidence grows greater and greater that even the common people of the Church, so long as they had not fallen a prey to sectarianism or been touched by radical humanism, were genuinely devoted to their Catholic faith despite all the abuses, and that daily life remained embedded in religious usage right up to the end of the Middle Ages. Even the simple people then knew how to distinguish between the office and the person's own piety and to apply our Lord's words to the gloomy contemporary scene: "So you must obey them and do everything they tell you. But do not do what they do, for they do not practice what they preach" (Matt. 23.3).

During this same second half of the fifteenth century, there was an abundance of pious works *ad remedium animae* (for the welfare of souls): new churches were built, new parishes opened, new appointments of preachers made and charitable institutions set up. New religious and brotherhoods were formed, and even new devotions introduced, such as the *Angelus*[26] and the Way of the Cross.[27] There was more catechetical and devotional literature than ever. Booklets and examinations of conscience for Confession, catechism tables, Bible storybooks, rhymed Bibles, poor men's Bibles, appeared in the service of religious instruction. Before 1518 a translation of the Bible into High German had run into fourteen editions and one in Low German into four editions. All in all one can fairly speak of an increase of piety in this period. Yet it was seriously lacking in the inner spirit, in the living penetration of pious practices with the spirit of the Gospel. There was too much externalism, too much mere automatism and superficiality, and also far too much unhealthy emotionalism in this piety.

The shepherds and teachers who might have directed and deepened the stream of faith were lacking. The higher clergy were mostly noblemen who had entered the priesthood from material rather than spiritual motives. Bishoprics, prelacies and abbacies had for long been the preserve of the nobility. At the outbreak of the Reformation eighteen bishoprics and arch-bishoprics in Germany were occupied by the sons of princes. Proof of proficiency in the tourney was an absolutely requisite qualification for most canonries. It is evident that prelates so immersed in worldliness and pleasure had neither the ability nor the desire to break the Bread of Life to the people.

Over against these prelates, "God's Junkers," we see the lower clergy. They seldom had benefices of their own and were compelled either to carry out the duties of a benefice for a pittance from some member of the higher clergy, or earn their living by helping to serve Mass and doing odd jobs about the church. Their economic position was therefore extremely precarious. Their theological training was no better. Excepting the handful of the clergy who were educated at the universities, most of them contented themselves with a modest smattering of religion, Latin and liturgy. Their morals were not much better than their theological knowledge. One could hardly expect a higher moral standard from them than the example set by their superiors.

Documentary evidence indicates that there was amongst them much brutality, drunkenness, gambling, avarice, simony and superstition. To secure a living for themselves they exact-ed almost insupportable fees for the slightest exercise of their priesthood, even from the poor and destitute. The charge for the administration of the Last Sacraments was so high that Extreme Unction[28] was called "the Sacrament of the rich." Concubinage was so general that at the Councils of Constance and Basle the Emperor Sigismund [lived 1361-1437] pro-posed the abolition of the law of celibacy.

Amidst the general decline there were still of course plenty of morally upright priests. The humanist Jakob Wimpfeling, a severely critical observer of the life of the Church, vouched "before God" to knowing in the six dioceses of the Rhine "many, nay innumerable, chaste and learned prelates and clergy, of unblemished reputation, full of piety, liberality and care for the poor" (Lortz, vol. i, p.90). We need only call to mind the illustrious figure of the saintly Nicholas of Cusa,* the herald of the modern age and tireless reformer, who sought over and over again by visitations, by word of mouth, and in his writings, to communicate his own spirit of piety to the German Church. But to most of the clergy we must apply the words of Pope Adrian VI [1522-1523] in his first consistorial address, quoting from St. Bernard: "Vice has grown so much a matter of course that those who are stained with it are no longer aware of the stink of sin."

The regular clergy were no better than the seculars.[29] Here too we must, of course, beware of false generalizations. It was precisely in this second half of the fifteenth century that almost all the older Orders made an effort to reform. In the case of the Benedictines there were, for example, the reforms of Kastl, Melk and Bursfeld. All the Mendicant Orders[30] still had houses in which the original lofty spirit of the love of God and neighbor was alive. And again and again a saint would arise somewhere in the Church, like Bernardino of Siena, John Capistran the lover of souls, and the noble Caritas Pirkheimer, who were shining examples of Christian piety. Luther's account of his own experiences in the Augustinian Priory at Erfurt gives the lie to the statement that monastic discipline was in a universal decline. It is also significant that later on it was ex-monks in particular who were among Luther's best co-operators—who were among the most impatient, in fact, of current abuses.

Nevertheless, we have from within the Church enough official and unofficial testimony to give us a gloomy picture of life in the Orders. Amongst the more ancient Orders only the Carthusians and in part the Cistercians really maintained their original standard. In the other monasteries there was a tragic decline in discipline.

The great Benedictine abbeys had become a mere convenience of the nobility. But in the Mendicant Orders, too, the foundations of the religious life had begun to totter—not least on account of the irresponsible caprice with which the officials of the Curia at Avignon dispensed religious from the existing rules of the Order or abolished them altogether. Monks and nuns outside the cloister were already a familiar sight in the fifteenth century, and in the sixteenth the begging friars obtained general permission from Rome to live outside their priories. Community life, and especially community prayer, fell into disuse. So did voluntary poverty. Many of the monks retained their inherited estates and bought or inherited their own cells in the monastery. Erasmus of Rotterdam* in his *Enchiridion* singles out for blame their lovelessness and their avarice. Other moral transgressions must be added. The Béguines,[31] for instance, had won for themselves the nickname of "the Friars' cellaresses." The sister of Duke Magnus was known among the rich Clares of Ribnitz as *impudicissima abbatissa* [the unchaste abbess].

It is not to be wondered at that the "Shavenheads," as the monks were called, were despised and hated by the people, all the more because they were patently increasing in numbers. Together with the lower clergy and the wandering scholars, the "stormy petrels of the revolution," they formed a clerical proletariat. Johannes Agricola* estimated the total number of clergy and religious in Germany at the time—in a small total population—at one million four hundred thousand (Lortz, vol. i, p. 86). It cannot be doubted that the majority of this clerical proletariat had neither the intellectual nor the moral capacity to so much as guess the profundity of the questions raised by Luther, let alone fully to realize the gravity of the challenge and to counter it with an adequate response.

*Omne malum a clero*—every evil comes from the clergy. As early as 1245 at the Council of Lyons, Pope Innocent IV

[1243-1254] had called the sins of the higher and lower clergy one of the five wounds in the Body of the Church, and at the second Council of Lyons in 1274 Pope Gregory X [1271-1276] declared that the wickedness of many prelates was the cause of the ruin of the whole world (cf. Bihlmeyer, vol. ii, p. 336). Machiavelli,* again, speaks volumes in the sarcastic remark that "We Italians may thank the Church and our priests that we have become irreligious and wicked" (Lortz, vol. i, p. 119).

### Relics, Indulgences, Pilgrimages

In this waste of clerical corruption it was impossible for the spirit of our Lord to penetrate into the people, take root there and bring true religion to flower. Since there was at this time no catechism of infants, the sermons on Sundays and feast-days were the chief sources from which the laity drew their religious education. And these sources were often choked up. Since at this time, moreover, as during the whole of the Middle Ages, Communion[32] was very infrequent outside the ranks of the mystics, there was no sacramental impulse towards an interiorizing and deepening of religion. So the attention of the faithful was directed towards externals. Religion was materialized. Pious interest was focused more on the "holy things"—relics[33]—than on the sacraments, more on pilgrimages and flagellations than on attending the services of the Church, and most of all on indulgences.[34]

The seeking of relics and indulgences had grown to gigantic proportions since Leo X had attached indulgences of a thousand, ten thousand and a hundred thousand years to the veneration of relics. Erasmus criticized this kind of piety in the bitter words: "We kiss the shoes of the saints and their dirty kerchiefs while we leave their writings, their holiest and truest relics, to lie unread" (Lortz, vol. i, p. 108). Frederick the Wise, the famous protector of Luther, had built up his treasury of relics in the Castle Church at Wittenburg to 18,885 fragments. Anyone who believed in and venerated them could gain indulgences amounting to two million years. When Boniface IX made of ecclesiastical indulgences what looked like a commercial traffic, even secular princes and cities became eager to take part in the distribution of them, so as to assure for themselves a generous share of the inflowing money.[Ψ]

From the middle of the fifteenth century the Popes began to distribute indulgences for the dead. The Legate[35] Peraudi, in connection with an indulgence granted by Pope Sixtus IV to Louis XI for the whole of France, announced that the indulgence could be made *certainly* effective for any soul in purgatory, even if the person gaining it were in a state of mortal sin, so long as the indulgenced work (i.e., money payment) were performed. Sixtus IV did indeed correct his legate's declaration to the extent of saying that the application of the indulgence to the dead could only be a matter of *petition*, not of certainty. But Peraudi's other statement—that the indulgence could be gained for the dead by people living in mortal sin—was never censured.

In the prevailing low state of clerical education, preachers of the indulgence (such as the Dominican Tetzel* for instance) eagerly seized on Peraudi's pronouncement, so that many preachers really did adopt as their favorite tag: "Your cash no sooner clinks in the bowl than out of purgatory jumps the soul." Some of the papal decrees themselves were in great measure responsible for this crude interpretation of

---

[Ψ] The Jubilee Indulgence of 1390 was extended to various cities besides Rome. A condition for gaining it was a money payment, collected by bankers appointed in the different towns who retained half the sum collected as a commission. See Vansteenberghe, article "Boniface IX" in the *Dictionnaire d'histoire et de géographie ecclésiastique*, vol. ix (1937), p. 919. (Trans.)

indulgences. They employed a misleading formula current from the thirteenth century onwards which spoke of a *remissio a poena et culpa* (remission of pain and guilt) or even of a *remissio peccatorum* (remission of sins),$^{\Psi}$ whereas an indulgence is not concerned with the forgiveness of the guilt of sin, nor with the remission of eternal punishment, but only with the remission of temporal punishment, that is, a mitigation or shortening of that penitential suffering which the sinner must undergo either here or in purgatory.

It is unnecessary to emphasize how much this hideous simoniacal abuse of indulgences corrupted true piety, and how indulgences were perverted to a blasphemous haggling with God. Night fell on the German Church, a night that grew ever deeper and darker as other abuses attached themselves to the excessive veneration of relics and the practice of indulgences. The latter was encouraged by the current mass-pilgrimages which were positively epidemic. Associated with them, especially at the time of the Great Schism, was the movement of the flagellants,[36] in which pilgrimage was combined with public self-scourging. Though condemned alike by Pope Clement VI [1342-1352] and the Council of Constance they constantly reasserted themselves, uprooted the faithful from their proper situation in parochial and domestic life, and threw them into a state of hysterical excess and unhealthy mysticism.

Behind all these excesses was the driving power of rampant superstition. Allying itself with religion, it had taken possession of the broad mass of the people. It is probably true to say that this superstition had made itself even more at home in the

---

$^{\Psi}$ These phrases were intended to refer, not only to the indulgence, but to the repentance and absolution that went before it as well. But from the Jubilee of 1390 onwards confessors and preachers of indulgences often failed entirely to refer to the necessity of repentance. See Vansteenberghe, loc. Cit. (Trans.)

German soul than elsewhere, and developed, even amongst educated people, a vast obsession with the devil. It was a lingering heritage from Germanic and Roman paganism. Since the Inquisition's[37] campaign against the Catharists,[38] who had acknowledged Evil as a first principle, this devil-obsession had begun to ruin daily living and social intercourse. In particular, there was a totally uncritical acceptance of every kind of improbable horror charged against witches. The witch-trials and witch-burnings went on—by inquisitors, secular governments, the reformers (Luther himself taught that witches must be destroyed)—and the official Church did not shield the victims of these atrocities with the bulwark of clear Gospel teaching. On the contrary, Innocent VIII, in his Bull *Summis desiderantes* (1484), gave the Dominicans in Constance plenary powers in the matter of witch-burning, and threatened with ecclesiastical punishments anyone who opposed the prosecution of witches. He thus did all that the highest ecclesiastical authority could do to encourage and legalize the obsession. Christ had healed those possessed by devils, but now, in the name of the same Christ, they were to be burnt.

### "And it was night"

It was night indeed in a great part of Christendom. Such is the conclusion of our survey of the end of the fifteenth century: amongst the common people, a fearful decline of true piety into religious materialism and morbid hysteria; amongst the clergy, both lower and higher, widespread worldliness and neglect of duty; and amongst the very Shepherds of the Church, demonic ambition and sacrilegious perversion of holy things. Both clergy and people must cry *mea culpa, mea maxima culpa*! [I am culpable, I am most culpable.]

Yes, it was night. Had Martin Luther then arisen with his marvelous gifts of mind and heart, his warm penetration of the essence of Christianity, his passionate defiance of all unholiness

25

and ungodliness, the elemental fury of his religious experience, his surging, soul-shattering power of speech, and not least that heroism in the face of death with which he defied the powers of this world—had he brought all these magnificent qualities to the removal of the abuses of the time and the cleansing of God's garden from weeds, had he remained a faithful member of his Church, humble and simple, sincere and pure, then indeed we should today be his grateful debtors. He would be forever our great Reformer, our true man of God, our teacher and leader, comparable to Thomas Aquinas and Francis of Assisi. He would have been the greatest saint of the German people, the refounder of the Church in Germany, a second Boniface...

But—and here lies the tragedy of the Reformation and of German Christianity—he let the warring spirits drive him to overthrow not merely the abuses in the Church, but the Church Herself, founded upon Peter, bearing through the centuries the *successio apostolica*; he let them drive him to commit what St. Augustine called the greatest sin with which a Christian can burden himself:[39] he set up altar against altar and tore in pieces the one Body of Christ.

How did this come about? And must we continue for ever to join in that lament of contemporary Christendom which St. Augustine sounded in his work against the Donatists, *Ego laceror valde* (cruelly am I torn)? These are questions which I shall seek to answer.

# CHAPTER TWO

# Luther

When we pass in review these abuses in the government and people of the Church, the conviction is borne in upon us that everything points to an imminent storm. The angry clamor for a reform in Head and members could be silenced no longer.

But to speak of a *reform of the Head* was an unmistakable indication that people in Germany were not thinking of discarding the Head of the Church, but of improving him. Apart from a few groups of radical humanists and sectarians, the universal detestation was not for the Pope as the divinely instituted guarantee of the Church's unity, not for the religious authority of the Papal See, but only for the utter worldliness of the Popes and the Curia. The desire of all was to have at Rome a real representative of Christ, breathing the spirit of Christ in his person and activity.

And when speaking of a reform of the members, no one thought for a moment of revolutionary changes in the nature of the Church. There was no desire to alter the substance of dogma, the form of worship or ecclesiastical government, only to abolish all the obvious aberrations and distortions of the Church's inner life and devotion. If we avoid being distracted by merely incidental phenomena, and fix our attention on the whole climate of opinion which determined the spirit of the time, we see that the cry for reform was not anti-papal in any dogmatic sense, nor anti-ecclesiastical.

It was a simple, elementary cry for conversion, for total renewal. The conviction had penetrated to the lowest levels of the Christian community that this state of affairs could not go on, that the very heart of the Church was disordered, that, one way or another, a reformation must come. One way or another! As soon as the possibility was admitted that the change might come some *other* way than that which loyalty to the Church would demand, rebellious and threatening voices mingled with the chorus of the reformers, voices which announced, in the manner of Joachim of Flora,* the approach of an apocalyptic visitation and the violent over-throw of all things.

But all these voices went unheard. The Lateran Council of 1513 might energetically deplore the evil state of the Church in Head and members, but a really effective will to reform was lacking. In the next body of cardinals[40] to be created, those who were to be confronted by the Lutheran movement, it was still the prince-prelates of the Renaissance who dominated the picture (Lortz, vol. I, p. 193), not determined men of reforming spirit. And amongst the Popes of the succeeding period, except for Adrian VI, from Clement VII [1523-1534] until we arrive at Pius V [1566-1572], there was not one who seriously considered a reform in Head and members. What followed was therefore inevitable. Instead of a reform there was a revolution, a radical change in the fundamental substance of the Church and Christianity.

## The Final Break

The man who kindled the revolution and pushed on relentlessly towards a final break with the Church was Martin Luther. He was not merely the creator and head of the new movement. He *was* that movement. For that which the protestant confessions of today have in common—what we call today the "material principle" of Protestantism, its dogma of the exclusive activity of God and salvation by faith alone, and what we call its "formal principle," its acknowledgement of no other authority than that of Holy Writ—grew out of Luther's whole personal experience and is in its deepest origins his own personal invention. However much Luther may have resisted the dubbing of his own followers "Lutherans," Protestantism is nevertheless in its fundamental substance Lutheran through and through, Luther himself extended and developed.

How did Luther arrive at his new gospel?

The abuses in the Church were not the real *cause* but only the *occasion* of the Reformation. They found their culmination in the shameful deal in indulgences between the Hohenzollern Prince Albert of Brandenburg,* the Archbishop of Magdeburg and Mainz and the Papal Curia.Ψ The preaching of the special indulgence for the building of St. Peter's was allowed by the Archbishop of Magdeburg and Mainz in his dioceses only on condition that the net profit was to be halved between himself and the fund for St. Peter's. The Archbishop made an arrangement with the great German banking family, the Fuggers, whereby they collected the money. He thus repaid them the sums advanced to him to cover his fees to the Curia for his appointment to the See of Mainz and for the privilege of retaining the Sees of Halberstadt and Magdeburg contrary to Canon Law.

Undoubtedly such abuses aroused Luther to the point of coming forward publicly. They explain too why it was that the theses he nailed to the door of the castle Church at Wittenburg, *De Virtute Indulgentiarum* (concerning the power of indulgences), unleashed such tremendous forces in the German people. Most important of all, they made it possible for Luther to put the Church in the wrong and to justify his

---

Ψ See Philip Hughes, *A History of the Church*, vol. iii, pp. 501-2. (Trans.)

own doctrine as the one gospel of salvation before the mass of the people and before his own conscience.

Indeed, the longer the strife continued, the more violent became the clash of spirits, the more passionately Luther's hatred of the Pope's Church flamed up; and as he grew older, the confusion in his eyes between the abuses in the Church and the essence of the Church increased, his belief in himself and his mission deepened, and he developed an ever more convinced and more triumphant assurance that he was being summoned by God to overthrow Antichrist in the shape of the Pope.

Thus the abuses within the medieval Church certainly unleashed Luther upon the path of revolution, and justified him in the eyes of the masses and in his own judgement. But they were not the actual ground, the decisive reason for Luther's falling away from the doctrine of the Church. He himself, even, later emphasized that one should not condemn a man's teaching "merely because of his sinful life." "That is not the Holy Spirit. For the Holy Spirit condemns false doctrine and is patient with the weak in faith, as is taught in Romans 14.15, and everywhere in Paul. I would have little against the Papists if they taught true doctrine. Their evil life would do no great harm." (Lortz, vol. I, p. 390.)

It was not ecclesiastical abuses that made him the opponent of the Catholic Church, but the conviction that she was *teaching* falsely. And this conviction dates long before the fatal 17th October, 1517. He had interiorly abandoned the teaching of the Church long before he outwardly raised the standard of revolt. Certainly, as early as 1512, without as yet knowing or wishing it, he had grown away from the Church's belief (Lortz, vol. i, p. 191). How did this come about? In asking this question, we are confronted by the mystery of Luther, by the problem of his whole personal development.

## The Mystery of Luther

In reaching a judgement on his development it is necessary to remember that Luther, doubtless very strictly brought up in his father's house at Eisleben, was early imbued with a strong central experience of fear, an extraordinary terror of sin and judgment. This alone accounts for the fact that when he was caught in a thunderstorm near Stotternheim and nearly struck by lightening he cried out: "Help me, St. Anne! I will become a monk." He was overcome by a similar spiritual crisis at his first Mass. It was so violent that he almost had to leave the celebration unfinished. It is also significant that once, when at the conventual Mass the Gospel of the man possessed by the devil was being read, he cried out: "It is not I!" and fell down like a dead man (Lortz, vol. i, p. 161, n.).

These excesses of terror betray an unusual degree of sensitivity, stimulated by his deeply rooted fear in the face of the *tremendum mysterium* [fearful mystery] of God, which for him reached its most shattering clarity in the Crucifixion of the Son of God. Since his attitude to life was determined at its very roots by this fear, Luther was radically subjectivist. That is to say, he was naturally inclined to take into the tension of his own subjective consciousness all objective truths and values presented to him from without, and only then to evaluate their importance and significance. If any truth or value could not be thus assimilated to the thoughts already in the depths of his fearful soul, he had no great interest in it. Thus his religious thought was from the start eclectic, one-sidedly selective. From the start it was thought overcharged with feeling, enveloped by a secret fear and laboring under the tormenting question: how am I to find a merciful God? From the start the primary object of his thought was to release the tension in his own soul, to deliver himself, to bring tranquility to his distraught spirit. Always the stress was on *I*, everything pivoting on his own experience.

On the other hand, it cannot be doubted, in face of Luther's tremendous achievements in thought, decision and action, that despite this tension he was psychically healthy to the core. In everything that he thought, preached and wrote Luther betrays a robust vitality, an overflowing energy, an inexhaustible originality, an elemental creative power which raised him far above the level of common humanity.

With these predispositions, Luther entered the priory of barefooted Augustinians at Erfurt, probably against his father's will. Here he was to prepare himself, by strict spiritual discipline and hard study, for his future entry into the Order and the priesthood. The system of thought, the form in which all philosophical knowledge was then presented, both in the priory and in the neighboring University of Wittenburg, was the "new way" of Scotism,[41] with the stamp of its later Ockhamist development. Ockhamism had a decisive influence on Luther. He described himself as a member of the Ockhamist school (*sum occamicae factionis*). More precisely, he counted himself a Gabrielist, i.e., a follower of the Tübingen theologian Gabriel Biel,* who had adapted Ockhamism, bringing it more into line with the teaching of the Church.

From Ockhamism Luther received his anti-metaphysical[42] tendencies, his dislike of the Aristotelian and Scholastic[43] doctrine founded on the objective validity of universal concepts.[44] From Ockham too he took his concept of God. God is God precisely because of His absolute, unconditional will, His sovereign freedom and dominion, which is beyond any scale of values and by whose arbitrary choice alone this order of values was created. God is a God of arbitrary choice. He can therefore predestine some in advance to eternal salvation, others in advance to eternal damnation. [For more clarification on the Catholic view of the concept of God, and on the issues presented in the following paragraph, please see footnotes nn. 45 and 46 in Appendix B].[45]

Particularly important for Luther's inner development is the Ockhamist doctrine of justification. Pre-Lutheran Thomism, the Church's classical doctrine of grace, presents grace as a movement of divine love entering into the penitent soul and delivering it from the bonds of its fallen nature. In contrast with this, grace in Ockhamism remains strictly transcendent. Justification consists solely in a *relatio externa*, a new relationship of mercy between man and God established by God's love, by means of which all a man's religious and moral acts, *though remaining in themselves human and natural*, are accounted as salvific acts in the eyes of the merciful God. In Ockhamism, it is true, justification is still God's work of grace, insofar as human activity only becomes salvific by God's recognition of it, by His act of acceptance. But this recognition and validation does not in any way affect man's spiritual powers. It remains completely outside him and is simply seen and assented to by faith. Thus for practical purposes on the psychological plane it is as though nothing were involved but purely human activity, and as if devotion were only a matter of human acts.[46]

Thus the intellectual situation in which Luther found himself was insecure and threatened on all sides. Natural reality was not a harmony of truths and values, accessible to knowledge and fundamentally intelligible, but an ultimately unknowable multiplicity of concrete singulars, a world of confusion and riddles. And supernatural reality, the living God of revelation, is a hidden God (*deus absconditus*), far removed from any kind of tie, sheer creative omnipotence to which we are completely delivered up. There is but one way of escape from this overwhelming combined threat from above and below: blind fulfillment of the arbitrary commands of this arbitrary God as they are shown to us in revelation, the way of good works. It is a way crowded at each moment with moral activity, but for this very reason a perilous way, a way of stumbling and falling.

It is easy to see that the perilous and menacing situation thus resulting from the ideas of Ockhamism was bound to have a seriously disturbing effect on a religious sensibility already as troubled with fear as Luther's. The consequence was a series of crises, struggles and temptations. The readings from the Bible and from the writings of St. Augustine upon which his Order laid particular stress again helped to increase Luther's religious terror. It was in fact St. Augustine who, in his disputes with the Semi-Pelagians,[47] pushed the Biblical doctrine of predestination to the furthest extreme, going so far as to speak of a "reprobate mass" from which only a few just would be chosen.

Luther's first years in the priory were thus a time of interior tension, spiritual struggle and suffering. The hopeless feeling that he was not numbered among the elect but among the reprobate overcame him and grew stronger as he grew more and more conscious that he did not fulfill God's commandments in all things. Since he began early to condemn as sin every moment of natural appetite, even though unwilling, and since, with his exuberant vitality, such movements kept recurring, he supposed himself to be full of sin, and no prayer, fasting or confession could free him of this terror.

For many years Luther was thus visited by scruples.[48] "I know a man who believes that he has often experienced the pains of Hell" (Lortz, vol. i, p. 174), a sign of the seriousness with which he regarded his vocation as a Christian and a religious, and on the other hand an indication of how far Ockhamism had obscured the Christian gospel of grace. The strange and tragic thing in Luther's development was that, in his Ockhamist aversion from all metaphysics and especially from the "old way" of Scholasticism, he remained closed to the traditional Catholic doctrine of grace as represented by the great masters of Scholasticism, Albert the Great, Thomas Aquinas and Bonaventure. It suffered indeed a temporary decline in the late Middle Ages, but was taken up again by the "Prince of Thomists" Johannes Capreolus* and re-established in all its ancient purity by Luther's contemporary, Cardinal Cajetan.* Ockhamist optimism, in fact, in its practical, living results, bordered close on the Pelagian denial of Original Sin.

In contrast to this the Catholic teaching sets fallen man, man burdened with Original Sin and its consequences, in the center of the divine plan of salvation. It does not present salvation as a pronouncement by God's free graciousness of the justice of our purely human efforts to reach the redemptive riches of Christ. Salvation consists on the contrary in the grace and love of Christ, merited by the sacrifice of the Cross and penetrating fallen man, constantly washing away our guilt and supplying for our weakness by the sacraments and awakening us to new life in Christ. The fundamental attitude of redeemed man, according to the Church's doctrine, is thus not fear of sin and terror of damnation but trusting faith in the grace of Christ, which constantly snatches us away from all guilt and gives us Christ for our own.

If Luther had entrusted himself to this traditional Catholic doctrine of Grace, which his friend Johann von Staupitz, the Augustinian Provincial, constantly laid before him, he would not have had that experience in the tower which laid the foundation for his abandonment of the doctrine of the Church.

## The Doctrine of Justification

Luther describes this experience in 1545, one year before his death—fairly late, in fact. His other recollections were also made late in life, and contain a number of "foreshortenings" of various kinds (Lortz, vol. i, p. 178). So it is likely enough that a whole series of thoughts and impressions of a similar kind led up to this decisive experience in the monastery tower at Wittenburg, which was merely the final precipitation of them. In any case, a fundamental departure from the Catholic doctrine of justification is settled once for all in this experience in the tower in 1512.

As Luther himself expressed it, it was concerned with a deeper understanding of the Epistle to the Romans, starting with the Pauline concept of the "justice of God." St. Paul had written: "The justice of God is revealed therein"—i.e., in the Gospel (Rom. 1.17). Hitherto he had not been able to make anything of the scriptural words "the justice of God." "I did not love this just God, the punisher of sins, rather I hated Him." Only after pondering a long while "both day and night" did he perceive that the Apostle of the Gentiles did not mean by the "justice of God" active, judicial, primitive justice, but passive justice, i.e., that by which the merciful God justifies us by faith, as it is written: "The just man lives by faith." Luther immediately re-examined in this light all the related texts in Holy Scripture which he remembered at the time, and found that they were all to be understood in this sense. "Then truly I felt that I had been born again and had entered through open gates into the highest heaven."

Thus his experience in the tower laid the foundation of Luther's *theology of consolation*: Christianity is pure grace, not the work of man. It is in this sense that he interprets the words of the Apostle (Rom. 3.28): "For we account a man to be justified by faith, without the works of the law." It is strange that Luther should have considered that this interpretation of the "justice of God" was a completely *new* discovery, differentiating his exegesis from that of "all the doctors." In actual fact practically all the medieval exegetes proposed the same meaning for it. They all took the "justice of God" in the passive sense, as meaning a justice by which we are justified, which makes us just. But they did not draw from this the catastrophic conclusion that Luther drew and which, in his 1515-16 lectures on the Epistle to the Romans, he claimed as the true meaning and content of the Epistle: "In the Epistle to the Romans Paul teaches us the reality of sin in us and the unique justice of Christ."

This is the culminating point of his new discovery: man is sin, nothing but sin. Even the man who is justified remains *peccator* [a sinner]. What justifies him is the sole justice of Christ, imputed to him on the ground of his trusting faith. There is thus no question of the justice of any work of man. Man's part is merely to recognize his sinfulness in true repentance and, in this terror-stricken awareness (*conscientia pavida*), to reach out towards the Cross of Christ. It is God's grace alone which delivers him. As Christ himself was at once "accursed and blessed," living and dead, suffering and rejoicing, so the believing Christian is at once a sinner and justified. From now on Luther delights in thus putting the inexpressible in the form of a paradox: the believing Christian is at once a sinner and justified, at once condemned and absolved, at once accursed and blessed.

From the psychological point of view, Luther's total denial of any justice in works and his conditional assent to grace alone constituted an act of self-liberation from the fearful oppression which his moral life had suffered under Ockhamist theology and its exclusive emphasis on the human factor in the process of justification. From now on, he resolutely cast himself loose from *all* justice in works, from all human activity, and threw himself upon the justifying grace of Christ, thus getting rid once and for all of all scrupulosity and terror of sin. Now he is spiritually free: free not only from the exaggerations of the Ockhamist school with its over-emphasis on works, but free from *any* form of justice in works, including that which the Catholic Church had always taught; free, as he was later to say, from the *captivitas babylonica* [Babylonian captivity—imprisonment of the faithful].

He won this freedom through a series of arduous battles and defeats, in hard struggles by day and night. It is this that gives his new experience its inner validity and its tremendous explosive power. If he had attained to this new interpretation of justification by a purely speculative process, as a mere intellectual conclusion, an exegetical discovery, the matter might have rested there. He might have remained unmolested within the Church, since there were other Catholic theologians, of the Augustinian school, teaching something similar, and since no Tridentine dogma had yet authoritatively defined the relation between faith and works, or the process of justification. His new theses would perhaps have been attacked here and there, perhaps have been censured. He might have been regarded as a theological outsider, but he would still have remained a Catholic theologian.

But his expositions were more than mere academic treatises; for him, those ninety-five treatises nailed to the door of the Castle Church at Wittenburg mirrored the *Evangelium* [Gospel], the sole hope of salvation, upon which one could stake one's life; and the source of this feeling is to be found in those nights in the monastery, those hours of fear and agony when he burned with the fierce heat of his struggles for his soul's salvation. His new interpretation of the justice of God was sealed with his heart's blood, born of the dire need of his conscience—and for this reason it was infinitely dear to him.

All the defiance of his passionate temperament, all the unrepressed impetuosity of his robust peasant nature, the rich endowments of his mind, his heroic readiness to commit himself to the full, his immense creative power in observation, thought and writing, and not least his wonderful power of speech, beating upon the hearer in climax after climax and "fairly overwhelming him" (Lortz, vol. i, p. 147)—all these powers united now in a tremendous *sense of mission*, a conviction that he, he alone, had rediscovered the Gospel and was called to proclaim it to the whole world.

Armed with this sense of mission, which asserted itself ever more strongly and triumphantly as the years went by, he, barefooted Augustinian friar of Wittenburg, went forth against a whole world, against the Christian Middle Ages, against the weight of the world-wide Catholic Church, against the Pope and Emperor, and, not the least formidable, against the bronze ring of sacred custom with which men's consciences had for centuries been inextricably bound.

### Christendom Divided

Let me stress it once again: Luther's abandonment of belief in the Church was not a conclusion reached in the cold, clear light of critical thought, but in the heat of religious experience; indeed, his whole development was less a matter of intellectual insights than of emotional impressions. From the sheer intellectual point of view, Luther *never* abandoned the idea of the one true Church. His theological *thought* did not touch on the erection of a new Church, but on the renewal of the old. Even in 1518, when he had to give an account of himself to the Cardinal-Legate Cajetan, he declared: "If any man can show me that I have said anything contrary to the opinion of the holy Roman Church, I will be my own judge, and recant" (Lortz, vol. i, p. 393). And in the *Commentary on a Certain Article* in 1519 he commits himself, entirely according to the mind of St. Augustine, to the principle that one may not "for any sin or evil whatever that man may think or name, sever love and divide spiritual unity, for love can do all things."

But the world of feeling within him had been stirred to its depths; the violence of his experience overwhelmed all these rational considerations. The harder his Catholic opponents pressed him, the more he let himself be swept into a declaration of war against the whole Church. In his ninety-five theses on indulgences he had already questioned the power of the Church over the riches of salvation; in his Leipzig

Disputation in 1519 he attacked the infallible authority of General Councils and of the Church's doctrinal tradition and admitted as religious truth only what can be deduced from Holy Scripture.

From 1520 onwards he openly attacked the Pope as Antichrist. His address, *To the Christian Nobility of the German Nation*, which appeared in the same year, was, as Karl Müller* expresses it, "a trumpet call to seize all the possessions of the Papacy." And in his later polemical writing, *De Captivitate Babylonica*, of the Church's seven sacraments he admitted only Baptism, the Lord's Supper, and, partially, Penance, branding the other sacraments, together with the Church's teaching on transubstantiation and the Sacrifice of the Mass, *as captivitas babylonica*, a miserable imprisonment of the faithful. In the work which was the third main statement of the Reformation, *Of the Freedom of a Christian Man*, he portrayed the ideal of Christian life in the light of his new doctrine and sent it to the Pope. In this same year, 1520, as the public expression of his complete abandonment of the Church, he burned the volumes of the Canon Law and the Papal Bull threatening him with excommunication before the Elster Gate of Wittenburg. The Pope's answer was sentence of excommunication.

His break with the Church was complete. He went forward in the midst of a mass-apostasy of princes and cities, secular and regular clergy, nobles and humanists, burghers and peasants. There followed the Protestation of the Lutheran Princes and Cities against the decision of the Reichstag at Speier in 1529, which gave the new religionists the name of "Protestants." And then came the Reichstag at Augsburg in 1530, which, with its rejection of Melanchthon's* mediatory *Confessio Augustana*,[49] destroyed the last hope of a reconciliation of minds. Christianity in Germany [as well as the world] was divided, and has remained so until this very day.

## The New Rule of Faith

We must first reiterate the fact, admitted by all modern scholars, that Luther's departure from the Church's rule of faith was brought about by a *subjective* experience—his experience in the tower in 1512. As we have already said, abuses in the Church certainly strengthened Luther in this experience. They certainly armed him with his best weapons against Rome, and accounted to no small extent for the tremendous response of the German nation to his new Gospel. But they did not create this gospel; Luther did not arrive at his new interpretation of the gospel by looking at the deplorable abuses in the Church around him. He arrived at it by looking at the crying need of his own soul, the result of the conflict between the terror of sin which had oppressed him from his youth and the rigorous demands made on him by the Ockhamist doctrine of atonement. He was delivered from these straits by his experience of all-sufficient saving faith, the experience of grace alone.

It was a completely subjective experience arising out of the acute anxiety of his own individual mind, and it was so elemental in character that it not only drew itself into all similar religious impressions and dominated them, but also spread out over all his thinking and compelled him to see and accept only those truths which came in some way within the orbit of this central experience, and to ignore all the truths of Scripture which lay outside it. Only thus can we explain, for instance, his calling the Epistle of St. James, because of its emphasis on the justice of works, an "epistle of straw." Only thus can we explain the fact that he does not go in the first instance to Christ our Lord Himself, speaking to us in the Gospels, but to the written testimony of St. Paul, the last of the Apostles to be called, who was never an eye- or ear-witness of the life of Jesus. And only thus can we explain his complete failure to realize what interpretations and rearrangements need to be made to derive that doctrine of grace which Luther thought he could find in St. Paul from the most profound passages of Jesus' own teaching, the Sermon on the Mount, with its clear theme of works and rewards.

The subjectivity of his central experience can be said to have dominated his theology, determining the special way in which he read and commented the Bible. It is a theology of subjective selection. Luther was certainly not a religious individualist in the ordinary sense, trusting exclusively to the emanations of his own thought and to his own experiences when dealing with theological issues. On the contrary, his trembling spirit was confronted by the colossal reality of the God of Revelation, and the shattering impact of his Gospel. He knew himself bound to this mightiest of objectives, in the same way that he continued to accept ancient and medieval cosmology as final truth. To this extent Luther was, as Troeltsch puts it (*Collected Writings*, 1922, vol. iv, p. 286), "a completely conservative revolutionary." The word of revelation laid down in the Bible remained for him the unique source of all religious knowledge.

But it was not the objective spirit of the Church's tradition speaking and witnessing in the Church's teaching which interpreted this objective word of revelation, but his *own* spirit alone; not the *We* of the members of Christ inspired by a common faith and love, but his own unique, individual *I*. In this formal, though not material, sense Luther was always a subjectivist.

It is true that this subjectivism arose largely from truly religious depths, rooted, ultimately, in an elementary experience of the uncertainty and the helpless need for salvation of fallen human nature. There could be no greater mistake than to see, in the religious movement which had Luther as its origin, nothing but the product of a completely personal fear-psychosis. Luther's fear is the fear of all of us, the guilty fear of human nature enmeshed in the consequences of Original Sin. This alone explains why the Reformer's experience was, and is, capable of creating a communion. But on the other hand, neither can it be doubted that the special structure of this experience, its depth and comprehensiveness and its theological and sociological developments, bear always those marks of subjectivism which belong to Luther's singular, exceptional spiritual development alone, and are in no way common to humanity.

"Luther's great mistake in constituting his doctrine was that he took his own highly personal convictions, based on a very exceptional experience and perhaps valid for himself personally, and made them into a binding requirement for all" (Lortz, vol. i, p. 408). It was to be expected from the start that this subjectivist basis would be far too narrow and scanty to remain the standard interpretation of Christ for a whole world with its thousands of individual characters. Thus even in Luther's own lifetime divisions arose over essential points. Before his very eyes there took place a certain loosening and weakening of his doctrine, a loosening which left open at least the *possibility* that even the most differing sects might be able to meet each other in discussion.

The scholarly side of Lutheran Christianity, as much as its individual and even individualist origin, offers many things favorable to an understanding with Catholic Christianity. We must, of course, make it clear first that we are not considering the emasculated Christianity produced by the Enlightenment and German Idealist philosophy but *Luther's* Christianity, the original Lutheranism which he himself founded and built up. In a stimulating lecture entitled *What are Catholic Tendencies?* a leading Lutheran Bishop, Wilhelm Stählin of Oldenburg, has made a determined attack on that modern perversion of Lutheran belief which considers the "banalities of unbridled liberalism" born of the Enlightenment as the true essence of Protestantism. It is an attitude which thinks that the difference between Protestant and Catholic is simply that the Protestant "feels that he is only responsible to his own conscience," so that for him there is "no binding dogma and no compulsory creed," or at any rate, that he "pushes certain aspects of the Bible message out of sight or at least to the very edge of his field of vision."

Anyone who speaks of the binding nature of a dogma, of the presence of Christ in the worship of the Church or of a necessary ecclesiastical order is at once—so Stählin complains—accused of Catholic tendencies. In fact, he says with emphasis, dogma, worship and the Church's constitution belong to the "*true heritage* of the Reformation." And in reality it was "a sign of decline, a morbid symptom" when these ordinances were set aside in the name of the individual conscience. "If a man believes," Stählin goes on to say, "that he can sacrifice the fullness of the Christian revelation to some vague formless religious feeling or vague belief in Providence, he may hold himself to be a good Protestant, but in the true Reformation sense of the word, he is simply not a Christian."

To some extent this condemnation of Stählin's falls also on a type of Lutheran theology and a mental attitude which regards the liberation of the individual's conscience from despair as the essence of Christianity, and entirely ignores the sacramental *framework* in which this conscience has its roots, the holy ordinances of the Church. Of such a Protestantism it is true to say what Nietzsche* believed to be true of Protestantism in general—that it was "a one-sided laming" of Christianity (*Antichrist*, viii, 225).

Luther himself did not leave the matter in doubt; for him the Confession of Augsburg in 1530 was compulsory doctrine, acknowledgement of which was a condition of membership of the Church (cf. Loofs, *History of Dogma*, 4th ed., p. 748). So we are confronted, in Lutheran Christianity, with the recognition of an *objective ecclesiastical teaching authority*, with which every individual Christian conscience must come to terms. It is true that the Protestant conscience is more loosely bound to this authority than a Catholic's is, because the authority does not, as in the Catholic Church, rest upon the visible rock of Peter and is not visibly guaranteed by the apostolic succession of bishops. Looking at it closely, the Protestant conscience is bound to the collective mind of the Church as a whole, not to those visible authorities in particular who are the bearers and sustainers of that collective mind. Nevertheless, in Lutheranism too, Christian consciences are not simply sovereign, but obliged to submit to the teaching voice of their Church.

Indeed we might go further, and say that though Protestant consciences may be more loosely bound, the tie is not *essentially* any different from that binding the Catholic. For the Catholic, too, it is not ultimately the objective norm of the teaching voice but the subjective decision of *conscience* which has finally to decide on a believing acceptance of the revealed truth laid down by the authority of the Church.

It is really not the case that the faith of a Catholic is entirely accounted for by slavish obedience to the rigid law of the Church. He, too, is making a personal act, an act of reflective thought and moral decision springing from the deep center of his freedom, an act of choice. For him too it is an act that can only be performed in the conscience itself. Indeed, if his conscience, on subjectively cogent grounds, becomes involved in invincible error and he finds himself compelled to refuse his assent to the Church's teaching, he is, in the Catholic view, bound to leave the Church. The most eminent of Catholic theologians, St. Thomas Aquinas, expressly declares that a man is bound in conscience to separate himself from the Christian body if he is unable to believe in the divinity of Christ.[Ψ] Thus the two confessions meet each other both in their recognition of an ecclesiastical

---

[Ψ] *Summa Theologica*, I-II, 19, 5.

teaching authority and in the decisive place they give to the judgement of the individual conscience.

Furthermore, in their attitude to the Sacred Scriptures they are not nearly so opposed to each other as might appear from the formal Lutheran principle of "the Scripture alone." The Catholic Church re-affirmed and reformulated in the Councils of Trent[50] and of Vatican I[51] the ancient truth of the Christian faith that Scripture is inspired by the Holy Ghost, whereas modern Protestant theology tends more and more to admit only Revelation, not Scripture, as inspired, the bearers of the Revelation being themselves enlightened by the Holy Ghost, but not their writings. So that one can say that the authority of Holy Scripture is fundamentally better safeguarded and more strongly emphasized in Catholicism than in Protestantism.

Because they are inspired by the Holy Ghost, the Scriptures, and especially the New Testament, are always, for the Catholic too, the classical source of Christianity. They present, so to speak, the conscious mind of the Church. But the Catholic is convinced that the Church has also what might be called a subconscious mind. It consists of those remembrances, ordinances and traditions of primitive Christianity received directly from Christ but handed on only *orally* by the Apostles [2 Th. 2.15; 2 Tim. 2.2; 1 Cor. 11.2], which were not expressly formulated in Holy Scripture [Jn.21.25], although in the strictest sense they embody a primitive Christian deposit of faith [Acts 2.42]. This extra-Biblical stream of tradition must have existed from the beginning, since the first disciples, like their Divine Master, at first spread the Good News only orally [Mt. 28.19; 1 Pet 1.25], and it was by oral teaching alone that they aroused the faith of the first Christian communities [Rom. 10.17]. When they wrote the Gospels and Epistles, they already took for granted the existence of a living Christianity in the various communities, as the writings themselves show.

Nor is it of course the case that the Apostles and Evangelists were trying to achieve in their writings a comprehensive, exhaustive survey of the Christian message, a sort of early cat- echism. It would be hard even today to piece together a single, unselfcontradictory system of thought from the Bible without reference to the oral tradition. The aim of the Apostles and Evangelists was rather to *inspire* and *deepen* the religion of the Christian communities, always according to the different cir- cumstances in which they wrote and with reference to the growing problems which they encountered—not in any true sense to *establish* it. Thus not all the Apostles wrote; and again several of St. Paul's Epistles are lost to us. What brought the Christian communities to life in the first place was *oral preaching*, not the Scriptures. Again, we only know of the very existence of the Scriptures, and of what is included in them, by oral tradition. To this extent their authority is ulti- mately dependent upon that of the Church's teaching.

In the light of this overwhelming importance attaching to the Church's tradition, the Lutheran scriptural principle can- not any longer be upheld in its original form. On the other hand, we must remark on the Catholic side a reawakening of interest in the Bible, which has not only affected professional theologians but has become a widespread movement among the common people of the Church. Nor is there any lack of voices acknowledging Luther's translation of the Bible, with its vigorous language tingling with the violence of religious experience, as a classical example worthy of emulation.

It cannot be over-emphasized that those truths which are uniquely Christian, distinguishing Christianity from all other religions: the mysteries of the Three-Personed God, of the Son of God made man, of our redemption by the Cross, of the sanctification of the faithful by Baptism, Penance and Eucharist, of the coming of the Judge of all the world, of the Last Things—it is just this ground-plan and *center* of the

Christian message which forms the core of both our Christian confessions. Will it not be possible to find paths radiating from this center which will bring us to unity in those things which are less central? What divides us is not so much *what* we believe as the various different ways in which we take into ourselves and realize this one gift of Faith—problems about the nature of saving faith, the process of justification, the relation between faith and sacrament, the teaching, pastoral and priestly office of the Church. These are certainly matters of importance, and, for the sake of revealed truth, we cannot neutralize them or indeed yield anything concerning them. But they are nevertheless questions which would not, in the light of *early* Lutheran piety, be so involved and utterly insoluble as would appear from the religious situation today.

We must consider, for example, the fact that Confession and the honoring of the Blessed Virgin—two forms of devotion which a modern Protestant condemns as specifically Catholic—occupied an important position in Luther's own devotional life. Right up to his death he paid homage in his sermons to the Mother of God; right up to his death he went to confession to his friend Bugenhagen. "I should long ago have been strangled by the Devil," he acknowledges, "if I had not been upheld by private confession." It was the orthodox Lutheran theology of the seventeenth and eighteenth centuries that eliminated devotion to Mary and Confession from Protestant practice.

We should be even more struck by the fact that the "Confession of Augsburg" (*Confession Augustana*), drawn up by Melanchthon and approved by Luther, which in evangelical Christianity ranks even today as an authoritative confession of faith, makes no mention in its first part of any fundamental dogmatic difference, not even of the primacy of the Pope or indulgences, and in fact expressly declares that the whole dispute is concerned only with certain *abuses* (*tota dissensio est de paucis quibusdam abusibus*). And in the second part, where it enumerates these abuses, it names simply: Communion under one kind, celibacy, private Masses (i.e., the current commercial traffic in hole-and-corner Masses), compulsory confession, the laws of fasting, monastic vows and the abuse of episcopal authority; in other words, only things which in the Catholic view do not belong to the unalterable *regula fidei* [rule of faith], the sphere of faith, but to the *regula disciplinae* [rule of discipline],[52] the sphere of ecclesiastical discipline, which the Church could, if she saw fit, alter.

And even these abuses, as Melanchthon notes them, take on their repulsive, scandalous aspect only against the background of late medieval practice. Celibacy, monastic vows, compulsory confession, and the so-called commercial hole-and-corner Masses had been perverted from the glorious truth that underlay them. These detestable perversions will never return. The reforming Council of Trent tore them up by the roots. The evangelical historian Karl August Meissinger made some significant remarks in this connection in his essay on "Luther's Day": "If Luther returned today…he would find to his astonishment a Roman Church which he would never have attacked in her present aspect…Above all he would see…that not one of the abuses which were the actual occasion of his break with Rome remains in existence."

It is true that Melanchthon, starting from his urgent wish for an understanding, seems to have been too optimistic when he spoke in the Confession simply of "certain abuses" which must be removed. For it cannot be doubted that Luther regarded some at least of his objections as fundamental. But here too we must not overlook the fact that in taking up this radical position he still started from the abuses within the Church, and that ultimately it was his total opposition, born of his deep religious experience, to everything unholy, together with his volcanic impetuosity, which led him to make a clean sweep, to be done completely with all these abuses, and then to provide his destructive beginnings with a theoretical basis.

## Salvation by Faith Alone

We have already shown how even his principle doctrine of salvation by faith alone is largely accounted for by his resentment against the stress laid by Ockhamism on the human factor in justification. Since he was insufficiently acquainted with the great masters of Scholasticism, he simply identified the radically un-Catholic Ockhamist doctrine of justification with the teaching of the Catholic Church. When we look into it we see that his phrase "faith alone" is directly aimed only against the Ockhamist supposition that a man, once he is called to salvation by God's grace, can and must work out his own salvation by his own power and his own self-mastery. It was aimed, then, against the Pelagianism[53] lurking in the Ockhamist doctrine of justification, which made salvation dependent solely on human power. But it was not directly aimed against that other supposition, that man can and must work out his salvation *by the power of Christ*, that all human choice and action only becomes salvific when it is caught up by the grace of Christ.

It is a cleavage of ideas going right through to the heart of our conception of God: whether man is to be thought of as a completely autonomous, independent co-operator—or, if he wishes, opponent—of God in the scheme of redemption, or simply as passive in His hand, unable to work out his salvation except in grace and through grace. It is the latter which has always been the clear, unambiguous teaching of the Catholic Church. It was first actually formulated at the Second Council of Orange in 529 against the Semi-Pelagians, and repeated at Trent, illuminated by our Lord's image of the branch which can only flourish and bring forth fruit in the vine. Looking at it truly and profoundly, it was not against *this* that Luther raged and fought. His doctrine of faith and grace alone would have had its right place, its true significance, within the framework of Catholic dogma, so long as he meant by "faith alone" that faith which is active through love.

In fact, the phrase "salvation by faith alone" has never been alien to Catholic theology. It was in fact always Catholic teaching that we can only be saved by Christ alone, that it is only God's unmerited, unmeritable grace that lifts us out of the state of sin and death into that of divine sonship, and that even the so-called "meritorious acts" which the redeemed perform in the state of justice are only "meritorious by grace," attributable, that is, to the love of Christ working in us and through us. Insofar as the justification of man is God's work alone, we could speak with Luther of "extrinsic" justice. It is indeed also interior and personal. Luther too, in that same commentary on the Epistle to the Romans, affirms that this extrinsic justice "dwells in us by faith and hope," that it is "in us" though it does not belong to us (*in nobis est, non nostra*), that it thus, according to the Council of Trent, "inheres" in justified man (*atque ipsis inhaeret*, sess. 6, cap. 7, can. 11).

In the same way Luther's other doctrine, that the justified man is at once a sinner and just (*simul peccator et justus*), can bear a Catholic interpretation if we do not take it theologically but psychologically, if we regard justification not from God's point of view but from man's. In the first case it is indeed always a matter of Yes *or* No, election or reprobation, but in the second, it is a question of Yes *and* No, insofar as our hardest striving is always accompanied by some secret attachment to sin (cf. R. Grosche, *Pilgernde Kirche*, 1938, pp. 150 ff.). The Catholic too must pray day by day "forgive us our trespasses." Throughout his liturgy echoes the cry: "Lord, have mercy on us. Regard not my sins! Give us peace!" Even when the justified soul is no longer in a state of sin, it is still sinful. Every serious Catholic will wish and have to pray with St. Thérèse of the

Child Jesus*: "…I do not ask You to count my good works, Lord. All our justice is full of imperfection in Your eyes. So I will clothe myself in Your justice and receive from Your love eternal possession of Yourself."

It was the Thomistic[54] school itself which anticipated Luther's pessimistic view of humanity, since it taught that the capacity of fallen man to receive God's action is purely passive, which grace alone can arouse to activity and freedom. We can affirm absolutely that Luther's battle, fundamentally and essentially, was only with the Ockhamist perversion of the Catholic doctrine of justification, with an abuse within the Church, as Melanchthon rightly saw, an abuse which was never accepted by the Church. Ockham himself was arraigned before a court of the Holy Office at Avignon[Ψ] and kept in custody, until he fled to the protection of Ludwig of Bavaria; though the fact that the subsequent spread of his doctrine was tolerated gave the hot blooded Reformer a seeming justification in identifying Ockhamism with Catholicism and in denying, along with the abuse itself, its primitive Christian and Catholic background.

### Priesthood and Sacraments

A similar reaction against public abuses within the Church accounts for Luther's radical discarding of the seven sacraments and the separate priesthood. In his polemic *De Captivitate Babylonica* he expressly speaks of the multitude of human regulations with which the Church had made of the sacraments a miserable captivity for the faithful.

His own master, Gabriel Biel, had taught him, entirely in accordance with the Catholic interpretation, that in the Mass there is no question of a fresh immolation of Christ, but only of a ritual re-presentation of the one sacrifice of Golgotha, and thus that through the Mass the one sacrifice

---

[Ψ] But *not* for his teaching on justification. (Trans.)

52

of Christ is brought out of the past into our present moment, into our Here and Now.

Nevertheless Luther's violent rejection of the sacrifice of the Mass can only be understood in relation to that crude externalization, secularization even, which had penetrated even to the innermost sanctuary of the Church and, as Luther complained, made "the Altar of the All Highest into an altar of Baal" (Lortz, vol. i, p. 399). When the clergy were not paid sufficiently for saying Mass they used to say a *missa sicca* [lit. "dry mass"], i.e., they broke off the Mass before the Consecration. And when the faithful had a Mass said for them they often saw in it not so much the memorial of the death of the Lord as a kind of magic protecting them from earthly harm. As in the former case, Luther here identified a vulgar perversion of current practice with Catholicism itself, and made a clean sweep, rejecting the Mass as sacrifice and accepting only the Supper.

The same is to be said of his attitude towards those sacraments which he thought he had to reject entirely, especially Extreme Unction. As we have seen, it was called in those days the Sacrament of the Rich, because only rich people could pay the high fees for it.

As the logical consequence of all this, Luther rejected along with the sacraments those who dispensed them; he would have nothing of an official priesthood. It is true that his view of the priesthood of the laity was directly in line with his key-doctrine of salvation by faith alone. But it was not in fact because of such speculative theological considerations that he adopted this line and pursued it—he was not speculatively inclined, it was the rage of the reformer, wounded in his deepest religious sensibilities by the frightful degradation of the secular and regular clergy, that convinced him that the priesthood and religious state were in themselves the origin and bulwark of abuse, and that they must therefore be torn up by the roots.

But precisely because it was the abuses in the sacramental life that Luther had before his eyes, he never intended to attack the essence of the sacraments themselves, the idea of the sacraments in the Church. In other words, he did not mean to undermine the belief that heavenly gifts are exhibited to us and imparted to us in simple, earthly symbols. His confidence in the objective efficacy of the sacraments is all the more striking in that the subjectivity of his belief concerning salvation must have exerted pressure on him in the opposite direction. And yet he clung to their objective efficacy. He made it clear that he believed that the miracle of grace by which saving faith is imparted is performed in the act of Baptism itself. For this reason he accepted infant Baptism from the Church's tradition, although infants cannot have trusting faith.

Similarly, in deliberate opposition to the "Sacramentarians," as he called Zwingli's* followers, he associated the presence of the glorified Christ with the elements of the Eucharist; not, that is, directly with the subjective faith of the person receiving the Sacrament but with the objective faith of the Church, acknowledging the presence of Christ in these elements. When Luther, in his dispute with the Swiss Protestants, expressly taught that even those that are personally unbelieving or unworthy receive the very Body of the Lord, he was testifying in the clearest way to the ancient Catholic belief in the physical as well as spiritual presence of our glorified Lord. It is something independent of the faith within the soul of the communicant.

By retaining the Church's Sacrament of Penance—though without the obligation to confess and without the performance of satisfaction—by separating repentance from justification and holding that justification was only completed in the act of receiving the Sacrament, he was again giving decisive importance not to the trusting faith of the person alone but also to the extra-personal, impersonal outward sign. Thus a roundabout way was opened for the reintroduction of a kind of Sacrament of Penance, and as Harnack* sarcastically says: "A practice was created which was even worse, because laxer, than the Roman confessional" (*History of Dogma*, 6th ed., p. 472).

In all these sacraments it is a simple, visible sign that objectively guarantees the presence of the Holy One, the blessing of the Redeemer. Thus through them the Church's *functionary* who performs this sign in the name of Christ and by the Church's commission, necessarily in some sense re-enters the domain of the supernatural, and acquires in some sense full powers whose ultimate basis can only be an express decision of our Lord's will and a special commission from Him. Thus the old character of the Catholic priesthood still clings to Luther's lay priesthood, insofar as an objectively efficacious sign of grace necessarily implies a minister objectively and effectively empowered to carry out this sign.

We cannot escape from the fact that wide tracts of Luther's thought were simply Catholic. The people who eliminated these Catholic elements from his message were the Lutheran theologians of the period of orthodoxy, especially in the late sixteenth and seventeenth centuries. There have always been on both sides theologians who, instead of protecting and promoting living religion, have endangered it. On both sides it has always been their habit to entangle living beliefs in bloodless abstractions, concepts and ideologies, and then to use the result as a ball to juggle with in polemic dispute. And when, having elaborated their systems of thought, they commit them to paper, it is usually with bitter and choleric pen, and love is not in them. So it has always been. So it was then.

Luther himself, as we have seen, judged the doctrines, ordinances and usages of the Church according to their fitness for survival as he saw it: that is, according to whether they appeared to him to be loaded with gross abuses, or not. He suffered personally from the festering wounds in the

Church and sought in his own fashion to heal them. It is true that he went about it, especially in the latter part of his life, with a self-assuredness and a cheerful readiness to assume responsibility which sometimes bordered on irresponsibility (Lortz, vol. i, p. 427). He was sometimes too ready to simply cut off the diseased limb instead of healing it. But his fundamental intention remained the healing and renewal of the ancient Church, not her dissolution and destruction. In the midst of his most violent attacks on Rome he said: "I may be mistaken; I am not a heretic" (Lortz, vol. i, p. 393). In the depths of his soul he was still, despite everything, bound to the Church, and that means to the Church as he then saw her, *ecclesia, una, sancta, catholica et apostolica* [One, Holy, Catholic and Apostolic].

We find a very different attitude in the orthodox theology which gradually developed and established itself. It took the Lutheran doctrines out of their historical context, separated them from the ecclesiastical abuses with which they were bound up and presented them simply in themselves, as an abstract system of ideas, as the new Gospel in fundamental opposition to the old Gospel. Their expositions no longer envisaged the suffering Church, laboring under abuses, but simply the Church that had been. They were concerned to found and establish a completely new Church. Lutheran theology became radically anti-Catholic. It was therefore a special aim of their polemic writing to seize on all the Catholic elements which Luther had tolerated, and even expressly affirmed, and in the interests of the stylistic purity of their Lutheran doctrinal edifice ruthlessly to eliminate them. This de-Catholicizing process was pushed so far that today, as we have seen, Lutheran theologians who wish to bring their people back to Luther's own vision of the Church are accused of Catholicizing tendencies. Now indeed altar was set up against altar and Church against Church.

## The Papacy

But did not Luther himself, with unequalled savagery, attack the essential foundation of the Catholic Church, the "Rock" on which she is built? As early as the Leipzig Disputation[55] in 1519 Luther had disputed the divine institution of the Papacy and its necessity for salvation, and from 1520 onwards he never tired of branding it as "the most poisonous abomination that the chief of devils has sent upon the earth."

That is indeed so. Papacy had no bitterer, no more determined foe than the barefoot friar of Wittenburg. He converted opposition and even hatred towards the Papacy into an essential element of Protestantism. The Rock which supports and safeguards the unity of the Church became in his teaching a rock on which that unity splits.

It is so today. There is no greater barrier to the union of German [and worldwide] Christianity than the Roman Pope and his claim to have been called by God to be the Vicar of Christ and the Shepherd of all the faithful. All the theological difficulties that we have seen so far admit of at least a *possible* solution. But in this matter any such possibility seems excluded from the start. Why? Because in this matter not only men's minds but their very blood rise in revolt.

For centuries it was Germans who suffered most from the detestable strife which arose between the Papacy and the Emperors because of an unhappy confusion of religious and ecclesiastical issues with political and economical ones. The onset of externalism and worldliness which accompanied the Avignon captivity was and is felt by those of the Lutheran faith in a far deeper sense than by us Catholics. *We* make a sharp distinction between the person and the office. *They* see the crying scandal of a prolonged outrage against the majesty of the Holy One, against the spirit of Christianity.

Because their creed was born of the struggle against abuses identified with Catholicism, *protest* against the Catholic

Church is an essential element of their whole religious attitude, the necessary foundation of their independent existence. But even in those Protestant circles where religion no longer speaks with the accents of Luther, opposition to the Papacy is firmly rooted. There is no sense in hiding this. That passion for independent thought, for the autonomy of the intellect, which was engrafted into the German soul by nineteenth-century idealist philosophy, sees in every papal command, every Roman decree, every book placed on the Index, a relapse into the Middle Ages and a threat to the basic rights of the human spirit.

As we have already stated, there is no possibility of any Christian rapprochement with the prophets or believers of "free thought." They are too small and narrow for us, and, however much they rave about the freedom of the intellect, they are not free enough for us. They are too small and narrow for us because they shut themselves up from the start in the limited world of phenomena, the world of appearances. They put artificial blinders on eyes open to unconditioned, eternal reality, because they will not see the real world, the world of God, which brings forth the visible world and maintains it in being. Plato would say that one of their eyes is missing, the eye that perceives what is above and beyond the senses, the Reality of realities, the Mind of all minds.

We Christians cannot be content to share the vision of such moles. Even if the unfettered human intellect had attained to an understanding of all the forces and all the phenomena of this narrow little visible world and co-ordinated them in one system, we should feel in that system as in a cage. Again and again we should thrust our way through its bars to cry our *Sursum Corda!*[56] For we Christians believe in a final, supreme meaning of all being and becoming. This Meaning is the living God. And we believe that the living God has opened Himself to us, in certain *homines religiosi* [men of religion], the Patriarchs and Prophets, and at last in His Only-begotten Son;

that He has opened to us the very depths of His being and of His inconceivable love.

Standing within this love our souls can grow to their height and breadth. They grow free, incomparably freer than the purveyors of human freedom can ever become. For it is only in faith in the living God that we know that we are more excellent than the stream of cosmic forces and powers. We are above this stream, not below it. And it is only if we start from faith that we can read the riddle of existence and attain to the satisfactory understanding of the world and of ourselves. It is only because we are children of God that we are really free.

Union is only possible, then, where faith in the living God and His Incarnate Son still binds and strengthens consciences. It is only with *believing* Protestants that we can discuss this final decisive question: whether the Papacy was founded by the will of Christ, or whether it is Antichrist who has achieved an historical embodiment in it. For believing Christians this question can only be solved in the light of Revelation, only, that is, by listening in reverent fear to the Word of God, and to His Word alone, not to personal preferences and feelings. No anti-Roman sentiment should be allowed to decide the question for us or accompany our consideration of it. Ulrich von Hutten's diatribes against "foreign priests" are understandable against the background of the contemporary situation. All Germany was completely "anti-Roman" then, as the Papal Nuncio[57] Aleander was himself compelled to report. The policy of the Curia in matters of finance and official appointments, and other things besides, had exasperated national instincts in the highest degree.

Today there is no longer any just excuse for regarding the religious question from the point of view of national politics and giving it an answer in those terms. The Renaissance tendency in Rome came to an end, broadly speaking, with the frightful visitation of the *sacco di Roma* [sacking of Rome], when the Eternal City was laid waste in May 1527. The Council of Trent and the great reforming Popes, Pius V, Gregory XII and Sixtus V, finally eradicated the abuses within the Church.

Not one of Luther's accusations could justly be made today. Even the political dealings of the Roman See with secular princes have become impossible. No sober theologian would today accept Gregory VII's *Dictatus papae*. The Gregorian system, resting on presuppositions completely alien to our own, can be finally relegated to the past. It was a result of the medieval view of the world. On a deeper level, it resulted from the fact that the unity of Western Christendom was created by Rome alone, that its maintenance through the centuries was due solely to the authority of the Roman Pope, that the Emperor himself owed his numinous aspect entirely to his coronation by the Pope, and that it was common Christian belief that all matters of political, economic and cultural policy were from the moral point of view (*ratione peccati*) [with regard to the mind of sin] subject to the authority of the Roman See.

The rise of the principle of nationality and the national states cut away a considerable area from the Gregorian system, and it was finally superseded by the new idea of the world and humanity introduced by the Renaissance. In consequence it is not possible nowadays for a Lutheran to keep his eyes on the abuses of the late Middle Ages and speak of the papal Antichrist as a mainstay for his own religious position.

Since the Council of Trent the idea of the Papacy has been tremendously spiritualized. It has become strictly religious, strictly Christian, strictly ecclesiastical, and the glorious image of the Vicar of Christ shines out from all the illustrious figures that have adorned the Papal throne since the great reforming Popes. As things are now, the question of the divine rights of the Papacy can be decided for the faithful *only in the light of*

*Revelation.* Since the believing Protestant, with the over-whelming majority of modern theologians, cannot entertain doubts concerning the authenticity of Matt. 16.18-19, his conscience is clearly and seriously confronted by our Lord's words to Peter: "...I say to thee, that thou art the rock and upon this rock I will build my church, and the gates of hell shall not prevail against it, and I will give to thee the keys of the kingdom of heaven." He must face up to these words.

From the purely Biblical point of view it is indeed possible for him to think here of Peter *only*, not his successors or in particular his successors in Rome. But he will not wish nor be able to deny that there is another possible interpretation. For Christ's words are valid for all time. They are words of eternity. If the first generation had need of a rock if it was not to be defeated by the gates of hell, how much more would later centuries, threatened from all sides by schisms and heresies! Could Christ really have been considering only the few years in which Peter was to live? Would Christ not rather have been thinking of the Last Times which would be cut short by His coming and for which He wished to build an unconquerable Church? It is in any case *only in this sense* that Christianity afterwards understood Jesus' words concerning the rock and therefore called the See of Rome even from early Christian times the "See of Peter" (*cathedra Petri*).[58] For it was convinced that Peter died as a martyr in Rome and was buried there, and that he lived on in his successors. It was in any case precisely the Church of Rome which from the time of Cyprian (d. 258), Irenaeus (d. 202) and even Ignatius of Antioch (d. circ. 110), was regarded as the chief Church of Christendom, as its true and unique center of unity, creating and guaranteeing that unity.

As in the course of centuries the Church spread all over the world and the centrifugal forces, the forces of schism, grew stronger, so the inexhaustible vitality of the Church liberated centripetal forces too, and theologians understood more and more unambiguously and univocally the meaning of the Rock upon which Christ founded His Church.

There is a great significance in the change which took place in the attitude of the greatest of the theologians of the end of the Middle Ages, the Cardinal Nicholas of Cusa. Like many of the theologians of the time, at the Councils of Constance and Basle[59] he had, both in speech and in writing, supported Conciliarism, i.e., the superiority of a General Council to the Pope. But the lessons of Basle, the depressing realization that even the strongest religious desires do not prove themselves strong enough to create a unity of spirits, that there are situations so charged with explosive matter that even a General Council is no longer capable of reaching a united decision—all this drove him to the conclusion that amid the fluctuations of opinion there must be a last resort, a rock, to protect unity under *all* circumstances; a final supreme religious authority, which *ex sese*, i.e., independently of the judgement of the bishops, can decide questions of faith and morals, and to which the whole Church is bound.

What Nicholas of Cusa discovered was to be learnt in the course of time by the whole of Christendom. We find ourselves confronted by the facts that alongside Luther appear Zwingli, Calvin and Thomas Münzer;* that soon after Melanchthon's death the Lutheran Church was shaken by the crypto-Calvinists[60] and Pietists;[61] that in England, alongside the Anglican Church, Puritans, Presbyterians and Independents founded religious communions; and that today in America we can count more than three hundred sects[62] tearing the Body of Christ to pieces. These facts practically force upon us the Catholic interpretation of Matt. 16.18, as finally developed at the Vatican Council in 1870.

It is the *inner necessity* of the Church, the constant threat and peril to her unity from human subjectivism, that necessitates this interpretation. For the sake of the unity of the Church the Rock of Peter's office must remain through the centuries, so that the Gates of Hell may not prevail. Seen from this viewpoint, the Roman Papacy and its claim to Apostolic authority cannot be an insuperable obstacle to the Christian confessions' coming together. For it is this Papacy alone which makes possible and realizes what all of us Christians must strive for, spiritual unity amongst ourselves.

# CHAPTER THREE

# The Central Question Today

We can only speak in the full sense of unity in the Church if she stands upon *one* rock in submission to one shepherd. In the light of the development of the Western Church, this rock and this shepherd *can* only be the Bishop of Rome, whose See was hailed in the earliest Christian times as the *cathedra Petri* [chair of Peter]. Even distinguished Protestant historians like Salin and Kaspar do not attempt to deny that *belief* in the primacy, if not the *doctrine* of the primacy, goes back to the earliest Christian ages for which we have any evidence. The root of this belief is ultimately to be found in the early Christian view of the Church, in the conviction of the faithful that it was not they themselves, not their own Christian conscience nor their own interpretation of the Bible, but the authority of the Church alone that decided the question of salvation.

We have already pointed out that the first Christian communities were not founded by the written word but by the living teaching of the Apostles and their disciples, and that Christianity was already alive and flourishing before any Epistle or Gospel was written. From the beginning it was the *oral* teaching of the Apostles, not its crystallization in the Bible, which guaranteed the truth and clarity of the revelation.

From the literary point of view the Bible is a chance collection of missionary writings, inspired indeed by the Holy Ghost, but a chance collection nevertheless. It does not give a general view of revealed truths, a *Summa sacrae doctrinae* [Summary of sacred doctrine] in the scholastic sense. Only in the Epistles to the Romans, the Ephesians and the Hebrews do we find a comprehensive development of ideas. But not even these Epistles give the whole of the Christian Gospel. Several of the apostolic letters have been lost, so that we have, for example, almost no information about the first eleven years of Paul's missionary activity.

The *whole* of revelation, the legacy of faith (*depositum fidei* [deposit of faith]) was entrusted from the beginning not to literary chance but to the personal responsibility of the Apostles and their successors. "O Timothy, keep that which is committed to thy trust," Paul exhorts his pupil (1 Tim. 6.20). When the Gnostics[63] appealed to mutilated or invented written texts, the decision against them did not come from Holy Writ but from the "rule of faith" (*regula fidei*), that is from the living, believing consciousness of the Church as preserved and transmitted by the bishops. Luther's *exclusive* esteem and reverence for Holy Writ is in contradiction with the facts of history. From the beginning we find, welling up between Christ and the Scriptures, the living teaching of the Church, guarding and explaining the truth. Through every gap and rift in the Biblical message gleam the clear waters of the stream of tradition, coursing through the Christian communities, guided and preserved by the bishops.

It is indeed *Christ* alone from whom all the Church's teaching proceeds and to whom it all points. Christianity is Christ. The teaching authority of the Church can do no more than draw on the riches of Christ. The Church has only to testify to the Lord's truth, not to create it. She is not herself the Light but is to give testimony of the Light. The Church's teaching activity is thus not creative. She generates no new truths of herself. She only takes the old truths, objectively given in Christ's revelation (explicitly or at the least in germ), and brings them into the subjective consciousness of the faithful.

We have arrived here at something essential which differentiates the Catholic from the Lutheran concept of the

Church, and which provides the ultimate basis for the exclusiveness of the Catholic Church, her claim to be the one means of salvation. The believing Lutheran also recognizes that he is bound to his Church's confession of faith, to the ancient Christian creeds, to the Confession of Augsburg, perhaps to Luther's *Schmalkald Articles*[64] and to the formula of 1580. But there is nothing absolute about this tie: the believing Lutheran does not simply and directly hear the word of Christ in the teaching of his Church.

It is truer to say that he does without the formularies of his Church in his *own* experience of Christ, when he encounters Him in his own conscience. And insofar as this experience of Christ in each separate believer necessarily remains dominated by subjective impressions, it is in the last analysis the *individual* conscience that determines the form and color of each man's Christianity. His religious life does indeed gain something from this subjectivity—an interior dynamism, pressure and intensity; on the other hand it lacks any ultimate assurance, any unconditional guarantee that it is really Christ and His Truth to whom the believer has given himself.

It is a quite different matter with the certainty of a believing Catholic. He is *unconditionally* bound to the teaching of the Church, because he is penetrated with the certainty that in the teaching of the Church he hears the word of Christ. He thus identifies the Church's message with the Gospel of our Lord. However humanly inadequate, however conditioned by the times the formularies of the Church's teaching may be, they are yet for the Catholic conscience, in their deepest content, in their *substance*, brought out from the treasure of Christ.

In the strict sense this applies only to those truths which the Church expressly proclaims as truths of revelation. In the strict sense, then, it applies only to the realm of the Church's *dogmas*. But insofar as these dogmas do not exist in intellectual isolation but are connected both with each other and with truths in the natural order, the light of faith shines also upon their whole logical and historical context, and guarantees its certainty with varying degrees of intensity and logical strength according to the degree with which it is bound up with the dogmas themselves.

The other truths of faith which have been formulated in the course of centuries by the Church, though not clearly expressed in the Bible, are all contained at least in germ (*implicite*) in a revealed truth already clearly held and proclaimed by the teaching Church. They can all be shown to stand in an essential relationship to the Church's original, central dogma concerning Jesus the Christ. They have all, therefore, their assured place in the Christian message. They all had and have a salutary and creative effect upon the whole Christian body. They are all charged today with the devotion, the reverence and the atmosphere of living Christian faith. And we know that what lies behind all these dogmas is not the caprice of emotional piety nor mere historical chance but the clear teaching intention of the Church and behind her the message of Christ bearing testimony of Himself in her teaching.

We have come back to our starting point. We pointed out that the special character of the Catholic concept of the Church and the content of the Catholic faith lay in the identification of the Church's authority with the authority of Christ. The Church does not receive this authority indirectly, as though from the faith of the Christian communities honoring their Church as the teacher and witness of that faith. *Before* there were any communities with personal faith, and independently of them, when Christ founded His Church upon Peter, He constituted in Peter and with Peter the fullness of His own Messianic power. The Catholic sees in the office of teacher, priest and shepherd built upon Peter the continuation through the centuries of the Messianic authority of Christ Himself.

We must realize that, according to the testimony of the earliest sources, Christ did not attach this Messianic authority simply to the *personal* "pneuma" of His disciples, to their abundance of the Spirit. They were not His Apostles simply by virtue of being His disciples. For this they needed a special *commission* from our Lord. "As the Father hath sent me, I also send you" (John 20.21). This commission was given in the solemn act by which our Lord chose twelve from the multitude of His disciples to be His Apostles, exactly twelve, no more and no less, who were to transmit His Gospel to the twelve tribes of Israel. Thus our Lord organized the first Christian mission by the special call of the Twelve, the establishment of the college of Apostles. This college of the Apostles is so much the one and only organ of the full powers of Christ that after Judas' suicide the election of Matthias had to take place to fill up the number of the Twelve. The fact that within this college, as we are shown in the Acts of the Apostles, Simon the son of John occupied a supereminent position, and that even in the Pauline communities he was referred to simply as "Rock," is not due to his personal qualities, to the strength of his faith, for instance, but again to a particular, explicit *call* by our Lord, which took place, as a consequence of the strength of his faith, in that solemn act at Caesarea Philippi (Matt. 16.18).

The very first Christian mission, the first preaching to the Jews, was not only a matter of the outpouring of the Spirit but of institutional means established by our Lord Himself—the college of the Twelve and the office of Rock. And, in the same way, later on it was not simply to all Christians filled with the Spirit of the Lord, to all the men of the new faith and love, that the office of preaching the Gospel fell. On the contrary, unless an extraordinary charismatic gift gave evidence of their prophetic vocation, they must first receive *the laying on of hands* from the Apostles. It was only by this laying on of hands that they were numbered among the appointed witnesses of Christ (cf. Acts 6.6; 13.3, etc.).

Thus from the beginning the spiritual basis of Christianity, its striving for the fullness of the Spirit and interior perfection, was bound up with an *institutional* element, the connection of the plenitude of apostolic power with an impersonal super-personal act, the laying on of hands. This turns our attention away from the Self, from the personal qualities of the believer, and directs them to the authority of Christ, who alone sends laborers into the vineyard and from whom alone comes all redemption.

What was later called the mission of the Church (*missio canonica*) was from the very beginning an essential element in the Christian message. "How shall they preach unless they be sent?" (Rom. 10.15). Only by the form of the laying on of hands did the believing Christian become a missionary, a witness of the word, a steward of the mysteries. He bears the full powers of Christ, but not so as to be in any sense autonomous and dependent on himself. He is in no sense the creative cause of our salvation, but only, as theology expresses it, the "instrumental cause" (*causa instrumentalis*) and visible tool chosen by the Lord of the Church, with which He, our divine human Redeemer, invisibly communicates to the faithful the salvation which proceeds from the Trinity. The laying on of hands simply but effectively expressed the fact that the missionary had his place within the whole mission of Christ and partook of His powers. By this means he entered the "apostolic succession," entered into physical and historical contact with the first disciples and with Christ Himself, from whom every mission proceeds and who alone is its meaning and its object.

It is thus with reverent pride that the Catholic looks back on the long line of his bishops, for he knows that there is not one among them who could not historically show that he had been received into that apostolic lineage and so had entered into direct contact with Christ Himself. It is this apostolic succession of his bishops which guarantees to him that the stream of Christian tradition which brought forth and sustains the Bible is no wild torrent to break its banks and mingle with alien currents but that it was received at the beginning and conducted on its way by a strictly constituted channel, the unbroken unity of this same apostolic succession, leading straight back to Christ and guaranteeing the purity of the tradition received from Him.

Seen thus from within, the Church is primarily an *institution for salvation*. She is not simply a community of salvation, a community, that is, which receives in faith the salvation of Christ and carries it out in herself. It is she who *gives* this salvation and makes the faithful members of Christ. Thus she stands not only in a passive but also in an active relationship to Christ and the salvation He gives—always of course only as instrumental cause, as the visible earthly tool with which the Lord of the Church, who won her by His Blood, pours the treasures of grace and love proceeding from the Trinity into the body of the Church.

It is only because the Church is in this sense an institution for salvation that she can at the same time be a community of salvation. Her institutional, impersonal office constantly merges into the personal, the establishment of the Kingdom of God in the hearts of the faithful. The official side of the Church is never an end in itself, never self-idolatry, but always only a means and a *ministry*, a ministry to immortal souls. Simply because the Catholic sees in the Church's activity not the Church alone but ultimately Christ Himself at work, still teaching, still giving grace, still governing, his relationship to the official Church is a living religious thing, saturated with the same faith and the same love which he gives to Christ. What Eucken said of St. Augustine's concept of the Church is still true today of the life and experience of the Catholic:

All authority and every development of ecclesiastical power is sustained and embraced in intense personal living. The person in his direct relationship with God remains the animating spirit of the whole. Out from this life with God and into the order of the Church flows a constant stream of power, warmth and fervor which keeps it from sinking into a soulless automatism of ceremonial practice and activism. It is not the brute force of authority working by the sheer weight of its mere existence; there is an inner necessity insisting upon authority and sustaining it. It is chiefly out of these deep wells of life that the Church draws the immense power over consciences which she exercises down to this present day (*Die Lebensanschauungen der grossen Denker*, 9th ed., p. 241).

Catholicism means the closest possible fusion of the institutional and the personal, objective and subjective, office and spirit. And it is contrary to the essence of Catholicism when either of the two elements, whether the institutional or the personal, becomes exaggerated. In the balance of the two, in their organic relationship and interpenetration, lie the strength and life of the Catholic Church.

We must speak in more detail of this fundamental character of Catholicism if what follows is to be intelligible. The Catholic Church lives and breathes in the consciousness that by her apostolic succession founded upon Peter she stands in that stream of tradition which leads straight from Christ through the Apostles down to the present day. With this before her eyes she knows herself as divine tradition *incarnate*, as the visible embodiment of those powers of our Lord's Resurrection which are forever penetrating the world whether they were set down by the finger of God in Holy Writ or not. The Church has no need of witnesses. She witnesses to herself by the "divine tradition" in which she stands and by which she lives, indeed which she *is*.

Because of the way in which the message of Christ is thus united with her own tradition, the Catholic Church feels and knows herself as the Church of Christ in the emphatic, exclusive sense: as the visible revelation in space and time of the redemptive powers which proceed from Christ her Head, as the Body of Christ, as the *one means of salvation*.[65] Because she is aware of this she is bound to condemn all other churches which have arisen or may arise—insofar as they are *churches*, i.e., sociological phenomena and not merely a group of believers— as extra-Christian and indeed un-Christian and anti-Christian creations. To admit even the possibility that the final union of Christendom could take place other than in her and through her would be a denial and betrayal of her most precious knowledge that she is Christ's own Church. For her there is only one true union, reunion with herself.

Being aware of her mission she must, above all, anathematize the opinion that the true Church of Christ existed only for the first three centuries; that today it no longer exists, or at least is no longer recognizable as the true Church of Christ. And she is bound to reject absolutely the opinion put forward by certain Protestant theologians that being a Christian is simply a question of accepting the "fundamental" articles of the faith, even simply of accepting Christ, and not receiving in faith all the truths expressly or implicitly included in our Lord's teaching.

All these possibilities had already been advanced in the second half of the last century by the Oxford Movement within the Anglican Church, in the hope of establishing upon this basis a reunion of Christian churches. They all started from the assumption that the Catholic Church was not the one true Church of Christ, and that thus a union of Christian Communions must be sought not in but *beyond* the Church. And it was therefore necessary even then—in 1864 and 1865—for the Catholic Church, because of what she knows herself to be, to reject completely any efforts at reunion along these lines and to forbid Catholics to take any public or private part in them. The prohibition was repeated even more clearly in 1919 in connection with the World Conference on "Practical Christianity," and again in 1927 in connection with the World Conference on "Faith and Government" held that year at Lausanne.

To sum up all the past decisions on the subject, Pope Pius XI issued on January 6th, 1926, an Encyclical *Mortalium animos*, which set forth a fundamental doctrinal treatment of the whole complex question from the Roman Catholic point of view. Though he paid tribute in it to the religious and moral ideals which inspired these efforts at inter-Christian reunion, he rejected with all the vigor of his apostolic authority the assumption that lay behind all these efforts, the equality in matters of dogma of all Christian confessions. Such equalizing, he said, must necessarily lead to an indifferentism which would efface all truth and which would in the end reduce Christianity to a subjective emotional experience shorn of all the objectivity of Christian truth. The truth is that since Christ himself is incarnate Truth and reality, his Revelation too concerns objective *realities*, which remain eternally unchangeable quite independently of subjective experience. And because truth can only be one, it will not do to have Churches making mutually contradictory statements about the faith, although they call upon one and the same Christ. This means that the search for reunion is the search for the *truth*. This is why every attempt to achieve unity is such a serious matter, calling for a deep sense of responsibility toward God. Pius XI stated:

> Since the Mystical Body of Christ, the Church, is but one…it would be erroneous and foolish to say that His Mystical Body could consist of divided and scattered limbs.

Whoever is not united with it, is united neither with the Church nor with Christ Who is her Head (cf. M. Pribilla, S.J., *Um Kirchliche Einheit*, 1929, p. 224).

For the Catholic, in contrast to the Protestant conscience which is not in union with Rome, the *immediate* object of all effort at reunion can only be that each according to his powers should help to remove the obstacles which are keeping those who do not believe in her from the Mother Church.

For these obstacles are his responsibility as well. It is not as though it were only the non-Catholic Christian who was the guilty party while the Catholic could think of himself as completely innocent and magnanimously proffering forgiveness. We made ourselves clear in our first section: both are at fault, and this fault extends to Rome itself.

Pope Adrian VI made public confession of this through his legate Chieregato before the German Princes assembled at the Reichstag at Nuremberg on the 3rd January 1523:

> We freely acknowledge that God has allowed this chastisement to come upon His Church because of the sins of men and especially because of the sins of priests and prelates...We know well that for many years much that must be regarded with horror has come to pass in this Holy See: abuses in spiritual matters, transgressions against the Commandments; indeed, that everything has been gravely perverted.

And therefore he authorizes his legate to promise that "we will take all pains to reform, in the first place, the court of Rome, from which perhaps all these evils take their origin." When therefore the Holy See regards as one of its gravest and most urgent tasks the restoration of unity to Christendom—not only with the Orthodox Churches, which already have the essentials of dogma, worship and organization in common with it, but also with the Protestant communions—it is thereby fulfilling not only the duty of the Good Shepherd setting out in pursuit of the lost sheep but also the special duty of common penance and expiation.

# The Roots of the Reformation Fifty Years Later

*Kenneth J. Howell, Ph.D.*

A colleague of mine who teaches religious studies recently told me of one of his student's understanding of history. The student had been assigned to read a book on modern issues in Christianity published in 1981. After reading the book the student asked the professor, "Well, when are we going to read the modern stuff?" My colleague felt justly disheartened at the student's sense of history. If issues addressed in 1981 could be considered pre-modern, the writings of a German theologian from the 1940s must be positively Neanderthal.

Extreme though this incident may seem, it is not far from many Americans' deficient sense of history. For many American Christians, the issues of the Protestant Reformation are now four centuries old and are thereby irrelevant to "modern concerns." But even a nodding acquaintance with the issues of the Reformation makes us realize the relevance of history. What may surprise some is that Reformation history is as relevant to Catholics as it is to Protestants. One of the great Catholic theologians of the twentieth century, Karl Adam, shows us the engaging force of history. The history of the Reformation and the divisions in western Christendom over the last four hundred years demonstrate the living reality of history in two senses. The teachings of the founders of various movements live on in the hearts of their disciples today, and the memories of past injustices and failures often bar the way of reunion among Protestants and Catholics.

When Karl Adam wrote *The Roots of the Reformation* around the middle of the twentieth century, he did so in response to a movement in Germany that placed the reunion of Catholics and Protestants in bold relief. This movement, called *Una Sancta*, built itself on the conscious attempt to return to the roots of ancient Christianity. The title of this movement was taken from the Nicene creed ("one, holy catholic and apostolic church") which both Lutherans and Catholics professed in worship every Sunday. This common confession evoked in the minds of many German Christians a call to heal the divisions within Western Christendom. In addition, the horrors and evils of the Nazi period in Germany's history called forth from Christians the realization that only a unified Christianity would stand against the social disorder of their day.

### Criteria for unity

*1) Seeing the need for unity*

The social evils of our day, increasingly prevalent since the 1960s, have had much the same effect on Catholics and Protestants in the United States. We are witnessing an unprecedented cooperation between them in fighting against the social evils of abortion, euthanasia, and sexual license. It seems that the disintegration of the society around them has moved Christians to address the need for a more united witness of the Gospel, much as a similar disintegration affected German Christians during the 1940s.

*2) Desiring unity*

Seeing the need for unified witness, however, does not solve the problem of how to bring about that unity. The problem of Christian unity often seems intractable. Even though many seek it, it always seems to be beyond the grasp of well intended efforts. Why is unity among Christians so hard to achieve? In a very real sense, the answer to that question is simple. To use the words of the Apostle James in his letter, "You have not because you ask not" (James 4:2). Unity must become an overwhelming desire for every Christian, a consuming passion that motivates each one. Our Lord Jesus commended the example of the persistent widow who pestered the judge to give her relief from her oppressor (Luke 18:1ff). A prayerful passion for unity, an intense seeking of the heavenly Father's gift provides the key. Unity among Christians, like every aspect of God's will, finds its answer in Jesus' promise, "Seek and you will find" (Matthew 7:7).

Yet desire for unity is not enough. We must know where the path to unity lies, and why we have not been able to find it. Karl Adam's *Roots* was quite prophetic, but even he could not see what greater efforts toward Christian unity would be implemented in the second half of the twentieth century. The developments in the Catholic Church since the time of Adam's writing indicate two pressing needs for the Catholic Church and all Christians: the need for divine grace and the need for repentance from past sins and injustices.

### 3) The need for divine grace

Our lack of unity as Christians derives not only from a deficit of effective methods or clever organization, but also from the poverty of divine grace within our lives. While honest and open dialogue is necessary, while organizational questions must be considered, in the end unity only comes about as a result of Christians being filled with grace. The teaching of Christ himself must penetrate more deeply into every Christian heart, for "Apart from me you can do nothing" (John 15). If He is truly the vine, the source of all grace, then we the branches must take our sustenance from Him. It is this grace of the Redeemer's divine life that will unite people torn by distrust and suspicion. Every layman, every priest, every bishop, in short, every member of Christ's Mystical Body must be "full of grace" (Luke 1:28). And it is in this need that we find Mary, Jesus' mother, as an example of believing simplicity. Her consent to God's will in her life (see Luke 1:38) provides a perfect example of how God's desires can accomplish great things when those desires live in the hearts of God's redeemed children.

The only way to become "full of grace" is to be nourished by divine grace through word and sacrament. If we had Jesus here with us in person, simply doing as He asks could immediately unify us. If we had questions of doctrine, we could ask Him and His divine judgment would stand. Yet Catholics and many Protestants believe that Jesus is here on earth today! All traditional Christians believe that Jesus speaks to us through His word, the Bible. The Second Vatican Council reaffirmed an ancient Catholic belief that the Sacred Scriptures are the very "soul of theology." This high confidence in the authority of the Scriptures explains the prominent place of the gospels in Catholic liturgy and in the liturgies of many Protestant communions. The gospels put us in touch with the historical Jesus who is one and the same as the living resurrected Christ. This same Christ is present to us through his instruction within the Church as the Church is fed on the Scriptures.

Christ is preeminently present to us through the sacraments. The sacraments provide us with an additional opportunity to be "filled with grace" by bringing us not only the teaching of Christ but also the divine life of the Savior. Why did Christ give us the sacraments and especially the Eucharist? He knew that human efforts alone could not achieve the will of the Father. Since we could do nothing without Him, He determined to give us His life through the channels of grace called the sacraments. The greatest of all these grace-filled instruments is the Eucharist. Since this sacrament alone confers the total presence of Christ (body and blood, soul and divinity), it has the power to unite all God's children wherever they may be. Our Lord founded the Church not only as an organization but also as an organism. And just as living organisms need food to grow, He knew that his Church could not grow into unity without His very life sustaining it. Catholics are constantly reminded of this at every Mass because each of the four eucharistic prayers currently in use include prayers for the unity of all. In the end, only Christ's presence in the sacraments can make us one.

## 4) Acknowledging past sins and injustice

When grace enters our life on an increasing basis, we are not only strengthened to do God's will, we are made aware of our personal need to confess our failures and sins. The desire for unity requires acknowledgment of sins, injustices and failures of the church and its members. Here is true hope for unity among Christians, and a reason for hope that Karl Adam could not foresee. This Catholic theologian, writing in the late 1940s, could not possibly have known what magnanimous efforts toward unity the longest reigning Pope in the twentieth century would institute. John Paul II has untiringly sought to bring unity to Christendom. His Encyclical Letter *Ut unum sint* ("That they may be one") attempted to extend and enlarge the vision of Vatican II by calling every Christian to an examination of conscience that genuinely desires to confess our corporate and individual sins.

Besides the doctrinal differences needing to be resolved, Christians cannot underestimate the burden of longstanding misgivings inherited from the past, and of mutual misunderstandings and prejudices. Complacency, indifference and insufficient knowledge of one another often make this situation worse. Consequently, the commitment to ecumenism must be based upon the conversion of hearts and upon prayer, which will also lead to the necessary purification of past memories. With the grace of the Holy Spirit, the Lord's disciples, inspired by love, by the power of the truth and by a sincere desire for mutual forgiveness and reconciliation, are called to reexamine together their painful past and the hurt which that past regrettably continues to provoke even today. All together, they are invited by the ever fresh power of the Gospel to acknowledge with sincere and total objectivity the mistakes made and the contingent factors at work at the origins of their deplorable divisions. What is needed is a calm, clear-sighted and truthful vision of things, a vision enlivened by divine mercy and capable of freeing people's minds and of inspiring in everyone a renewed willingness, precisely with a view to proclaiming the Gospel to the men and women of every people and nation (*Ut unum sint* no.2).

Not only do John Paul's teachings serve as a beacon light for unity. His actions speak even louder. Kneeling at the doors of St. Paul's Outside the Wall in Rome with Anglican Archbishop Carey and with the Orthodox Patriarch Bartholomew, John Paul shows that the path to unity lies on our knees. He knows that the posture of prayer and confession of sin will open the floodgates of divine mercy bringing a union of hearts that is at the very essence of the Church. This Bishop of Rome knows that the more we acknowledge our sin, the more the mercy of God will bring healing to the divisions among Christians.

Why has John Paul II raced to first place in his willingness to admit the past failures of the Church? His primary motivation undoubtedly comes from the confession of his own personal sins, and his profound awareness of how healing the sacrament of reconciliation can be. Yet, I also wonder if he knows something that few seem to recognize. Confession of corporate faults is probably easier for Catholics than for Protestants. This is not because, as one might think, Catholics engage in confession more often. Even though most Protestant communions do not have a formal sacrament of confession, only God knows who actually confesses their sins more. Nor is it even ours to inquire. I think rather that John Paul knows that confession of past sins, especially those against Protestants, does not do injury to the very essence of the Church. The Church is still "one, holy, catholic, and apostolic." The Eucharist is still valid and the office of Peter's successor is still the integrating and unifying center of God's people, even if Catholic prelates and people have failed miserably at times to live up to the splendor of the Church.

For Protestants it is quite different. For them to admit the wrongs of the past must necessarily cut to the very core of their existence, to their raison d'être for being separated from the center of unity in Rome. Karl Adam seemed very aware of this difference when he acknowledged many of the valuable criticisms Luther had made of the Church in his day. He sought to find reasons within the Church why the scourge of division had persisted so long. Adam also knew that he was on good historical grounds because he was familiar with the famous confession of Pope Adrian VI, made publicly through his Legate at the Nuremberg Reichstag in 1523:

> We freely acknowledge that God has allowed this chastise-ment to come upon His Church because of the sins of men and especially because of the sins of priests and prelates...We know well that for many years much that must be regarded with horror has come to pass in this Holy See: abuses in spir-itual matters, transgressions against the Commandments; indeed, that everything has been gravely perverted.

Karl Adam suspected that if there was ever to be reconcil-iation between Protestants and Catholics, the Catholic Church would have to take the lead in confessing the sins of the past. I think Karl Adam would have rejoiced greatly to see the spirit of John Paul's acknowledgment of the Catholic Church's failures. Perhaps he does even now. As the Church seeks to bring unity to all Christians, we of the *Coming Home Network* believe that the world has been given a great gift in these difficult times in the pastoral leadership of John Paul II. What Christian, Catholic or not, could not join John Paul in praying?

> Merciful Father, on the night before his Passion your Son prayed for the unity of those who believe in him: in disobedience to his will, however, believers have opposed one another, becoming divided, and have mutually condemned one another and fought against one another. We urgently implore your forgiveness and we beseech the gift of a repentant heart, so that all Christians, reconciled with you and with one another will be able, in one body and in one spirit, to experience anew the joy of full communion. We ask this through Christ our Lord. (John Paul II's Angelus Message for 12 March 2000).

*Dr. Kenneth Howell holds a Master of Divinity degree from Westminster Theological Seminary in Philadelphia, Penn. He also holds a Ph.D. in General Linguistics from Indiana, and a Ph.D. from Lancaster University (U.K.) in History. He was Associate Professor of Biblical Languages and Literature at Reformed Theological Seminary in Jackson, Mississippi for seven years, and served as a Presbyterian minister for eighteen years. He is currently the Director of John Henry Newman Institute of Catholic Thought at the University of Illinois.*

APPENDIX A

# Historical Figures
[compiled for your convenience by the
staff of the *Coming Home Network*]

**AGRICOLA, JOHANNES** (1494-1566), a German Reformer. In 1519 he served as Luther's recording secretary at the Leipzig Disputation. In 1527 he had a dispute with Philip Melanchthon on the relation between repentance and faith. Melanchthon's view, shared by the other Reformers, was that the moral law was needed to bring the sinner to repentance, leading on to faith in Christ. Agricola held that the law has no place in Christian experience. Luther refuted his arguments and elicited some form of recantation, but bitterness remained. In addition to theological works, Agricola compiled a collection of German proverbs. (p.21)

**ALBERT OF BRANDENBURG** (1490-1545), a notorious example of the multiplication of ecclesiastical benefices in one person. Before becoming Archbishop of Mainz (1514) and later cardinal, he had held two bishoprics and a number of rich abbeys. To meet his debts, Pope Leo X permitted Albert to sell indulgences in his diocese, the proceeds to be divided between him and the pope, and this led to Luther's historic protest. (p.29)

**ALEXANDER VI** (Pope, 1492-1503), reputed by many historians to have been the worst of the popes. Even though he led an immoral life, however, he never attempted to challenge or change any doctrines of the Church. His pontificate, beyond any other, demonstrates that the goodness or badness of the pope can exercise no substantial influence on the being, the divine character, or the holiness of the Church. Rodrigo Borgia (Pope Alexander VI) ascended to the papal throne by bribes and future favors to a majority of cardinals that elected him pope. He had mistresses, in particular Vanozza Catanei, who bore him four children. Arrogance, cruelty and ambition were his main characteristics; the pursuit of sensual pleasures and the enrichment of his family seemed to be his main occupation. After a heated quarrel with his brother-in-law, he caused him to be slain. (p.16)

**AUGUSTINE OF HIPPO** (354-430), a Latin Father and Doctor of the Church, a great theologian, writer and teacher. His voluminous writings massively influenced almost every sphere of Western thought in later centuries. (p.11)

**BIEL, GABRIEL** (1425-1495), a German philosopher, called "the last of the Scholastics," became a noted speaker. He was responsible with Count Eberhard of Wurttemberg for the founding of the University of Tübingen, where he held the chair of theology from 1484. (p.32)

**BRIDGET OF SWEDEN** (1303-1373), the most celebrated saint of the Northern kingdoms. She founded the Brigittines, upon receiving instructions in a vision. The Order flourished in Sweden until the Reformation. After moving to Rome she ministered widely to rich and poor, homeless and sinners, giving God's messages in a restless and corrupt age. She married and had eight children, but upon her husband's death in 1344 she retired to a life of penance and prayer. She was canonized a saint in 1391. One of her daughters was Catherine of Sweden. (p.17)

**CAJETAN, TOMMASO DE VIO** (1464-1534), a Dominican cardinal and philosopher. He held the chair of metaphysics at Bologna, and became a recognized exponent of Thomas Aquinas. He defended the supremacy of the pope at the Council of Pisa (1511). His greatest disappointment was his failure to persuade Luther to recant when they met on three successive days in Augsburg in 1518. He was one of Luther's most competent opponents. (p.35)

**CAPREOLUS, JOHANNES** (c.1380-1444), a Dominican theologian who taught in French universities. He was foremost in the revival of Thomism (philosophical thought based on Thomas Aquinas). His *Four Books of Defences of the Theology of St. Aquinas* used the sources systematically against critics such as Scotists and Ockhamists. (p.35)

**ERASMUS OF ROTTERDAM** (1466-1536), the most brilliant and important leader of German humanism, who wished to reform the Church through scholarship and instructions in the teachings of Christ. He eventually became a monk, and later secured the position of secretary to the Bishop of Cambrai. (p.21)

**FREDERICK I, OR FREDERICK BARBAROSSA** (c. 1152-1190), a German King and Roman Emperor, the successor of Conrad Hohenstaufen. Frederick's endeavor to restore the rights of the

German monarchy and expand his territorial control while reviving the imperial authority made him a controversial historical personage. He gained control over the German church, utilized feudal obligations to strengthen the monarchy, and enlarged his own family domains. He invaded Italy in 1154-55, repressed the Lombard communes, allied with Pope Adrian IV to oust Arnold of Brescia, and was crowned emperor. The alliance collapsed when Frederick firmly rejected the concept of papal feudal overlordship. (p.11)

FREDERICK II (1194-1250), a German King and Roman Emperor. His father had him elected king, but when Henry VI died the next year (1197), the princes refused to accept the youthful Hohenstaufen heir. In 1212 Frederick was again named king through the contrivance of Innocent and Philip Augustus. For the next three decades he found himself involved in a continuous struggle with the papacy. In 1245 Innocent IV excommunicated him and preached a crusade against Frederick which had little effect. The execution of Frederick's grandson, Conradin, in 1268 ended the Hohenstaufen dynasty. A skeptic in religion, Frederick was tolerant of Jews and Muslims. In his dealings with Christian and Muslim leaders alike, he proved to be a brilliant diplomat, administrator, and general. (p.11)

HARNACK, ADOLF (1851-1930), a German scholar, son of the Lutheran scholar Theodosius Harnack (1817-89). He was challenged by the Church because of his doubts about the authorship of fourth gospel and other NT books, his unorthodox interpretations of biblical miracles including the Resurrection, and his denial of Christ's institution of baptism. Because of this he was denied all official recognition by the Church, including the right to examine his own pupils in Church examinations. Nevertheless, he was a very influential Church historian and theologian until World War I. His main field of study was patristic thought. (p.55)

JOACHIM OF FLORA (c.1135-1202), Cistercian abbot and mystic philosopher of history, founded the Order of San Giovanni. He recorded two mystical experiences which reportedly gave him the gift of spiritual intelligence enabling him to understand the inner meaning of history. At times he prophesied on contemporary events and the advent of Antichrist. Joachim's teaching was not meant to undermine ecclesiastical authority, but it inspired groups such as the Spiritual Franciscans and the Fraticelli. (p.28)

**MACHIAVELLI, NICCOLO DE BERNARDO** of Florence (1469-1527), among the most influential of the Renaissance writers. He held diplomatic office under the Florentine government until the Medici came into power in 1512, when he was imprisoned, tortured, and banished. Machiavelli charged the papacy with responsibility for the spiritual deterioration of the Church and for the miserable condition of Italy. He attacked the medieval ideal of the relationship between Church and State, and taught that the secular state is wholly independent of religious authority. (p.22)

**MARSILIUS OF PADUA** (c.1275-1342), a political philosopher, famous for his work, *Defensor pacis* ("Defender of the peace"), which had a strongly antipapal tone. When King Luis IV seized Rome, Marsilius was named the imperial vicar of the city. Eventually he and Louis left because the people of Rome turned against them. (p.12)

**MELANCHTHON, PHILIP** (1497–1560), a German scholar and humanist, second only to Martin Luther as a figure in the Lutheran Reformation. A man of great intellect and wide learning, he was professor of Greek at the Univ. of Wittenburg when he met Luther, and they soon became intimate friends and associates. In 1521 his *Loci Communes Rerum Theologicarum* (Commonplaces of Theology) contributed logical, argumentative force to the Reformation, and after Luther's confinement in the castle of Wartburg the same year, he replaced Luther as leader of the Reformation cause at Wittenburg. Melanchthon served as a peacemaker because of his desire for harmony between Protestantism and Catholicism or for at least a union of Protestant factions, but his views were regarded as heretical by strict Lutherans. The breach was widened by his willingness to compromise with Catholics for the sake of avoiding civil war. He secured tolerance for evangelical doctrine; for a time he retained most of the Roman ceremonies as *adiaphora* (Greek, "things indifferent"), matters not of great consequence and therefore best tolerated. Melanchthon died praying "that the churches might be of one mind in Christ." (p.40)

**MICHAEL OF CESENA** (1270-1342), Minister General of the Franciscan Order and a theologian. He rose to the leadership of the Franciscans at the time when the Order was torn by strife between the "Spirituals" and the "Community" (see Appendix B, footnote 7). Michael's support of William of Ockham, theologian and apologist for the Spirituals, and his association with Emperor Luis of Barvaria brought about his excommunication by Pope John XXII in 1328. (p.12)

MÜLLER, KARL (1818-1893), a professor at Düsseldorf. He belonged to the more recent members of a school of German religious painters known as the "Nazarenes," who succeeded felicitously in popular but beautiful representations of religious devotion. (p.40)

MÜNZER, THOMAS (c.1489-1525), a German Protestant reformer, generally linked with the Anabaptist movement, although he rejected baptism altogether. He was an associate of Martin Luther in 1519, but his position soon diverged from Luther's as he became increasingly iconoclastic in theology and radical in political and social beliefs. During the Peasants' War (1524-26) he set up a communistic theocracy at Mühlhausen. He was later overthrown and beheaded. (p.62)

NICHOLAS OF CUSA (1401-1464), a German cardinal, philosopher, and administrator at Cues on the Moselle, in the Archdiocese of Trier. As a doctor of canon law, he wrote (1433) in defense of the conciliar theory that asserted the supremacy of church councils over the pope. Later, however, he reversed his position and became an ardent supporter of the papacy. In 1437-38 he was sent to Constantinople in the interests of reunion, and later served the papal cause in Germany. Ordained Bishop of Brixen (1450), he was appointed papal legate to Germany to preach the Jubilee indulgence, reform religious and diocesan clergy, and hold synods. Pope Pius II appointed him vicar-general in 1459. (p.20)

NIETZSCHE, FRIEDRICH (1844-1900), a philosopher and philologist, the son of a Lutheran minister. He showed early brilliance and was appointed an associate professor of classical philology at the University of Basle before passing his final exam. He went insane in January 1889. Charles Darwin heavily influenced his thought, and what Nietzsche took to be the nihilistic implication of evolutionary theory. Nietzsche attacked Christian dogma, but more especially he attacked the prevalent idea that Christian ethics could survive the overthrow of the Christian view of man which he believe the work of Darwin had brought about. He taught that "supernature" is not something that men have in virtue of their creation in the divine image, but is rather a goal for the future. The "superman," capable of self-mastery, must go "beyond good and evil," beyond the values of a defunct Christianity. (p.44)

**PHILIP IV (THE FAIR)** (1285-1314), King of France, whose political undertakings required large sums of money. He laid new taxes upon the French clergy, and it is claimed that in the reign of Philip, the Church of France was practically ruined by overtaxation. (p.11)

**TETZEL, JOHANN** (c.1465-1519), a Dominican monk, the first public antagonist of Luther. He preached indulgences near Wittenburg in the Spring of 1517. (p.23)

**THÉRÈSE OF THE CHILD JESUS** (1873-1897), a Carmelite of Lisieux, better known as the Little Flower of Jesus. She had a very trying childhood, including a grave illness. She wrote *Little Way,* for which Pope Benedict XV said it "contained the secret of sanctity for the entire world." Dying of tuberculosis, she wrote her autobiography, *The Story of a Soul,* the wide circulation of which has led to her extensive veneration. Canonized in 1925, she has been named patroness of foreign missions and joined with Joan of Arc as patroness of France (1947). (p.52)

**URBAN VI** (Pope, 1378-1389), Bartolomeo Prignano, the first Roman pope during the Western Schism. (p.14)

**VON HUTTEN, ULRICH** (1488-1523), a German Reformer and a humanist scholar. He was suddenly caught up in enthusiasm for the Reformation and the freeing of Germany from papal control. Bitter ironical attacks on the papacy led to an order of arrest from Rome in 1520. (p.17)

**VON KAISERSBERG, GEILER** (1445-1510), a celebrated German pulpit orator, noted especially as a preacher, effective in reaching the common people through his sermons. Although not a humanist, he stressed the need for reform and influenced Bishop Wilhelm von Honstein in his reformatory endeavors. Geiler has been called "the prince of the pulpit in the late fifteenth century." (p.13)

**WILLIAM OF OCKHAM** (c. 1280-c.1349), a scholastic theologian and philosopher, who entered the Franciscan Order about 1310. Ockham sided with the Franciscan Spirituals in their dispute with Pope John XXII. Ockham's ideas were not consistent with Catholic theology, and he eventually was excommunicated. (p.12)

**WIMPFILING, JAKOB** (1450-1528), a humanist and theologian, a Cathedral preacher at Speyer and later professor at Heidelberg. He led an educational reform broadening the curriculum, insisting upon the high value of the practical sciences. He was initially a friend of Luther. (p.14)

**ZWINGLI, ULRICH** (1484-1531), the founder of the Reformation in Switzerland. His approach to the question of public worship and his view of the sacraments represented a far more radical break with tradition than did the Lutheran reform movement. His own radical followers, led by Conrad Grebel and Felix Manz, endangered his alliance with the magistracy, whose support he believed was essential. Zwingli and Luther failed to reach agreement on the question of Christ's presence in the Eucharist. Zwingli never held political office. His influence was the result of his ability and personal connections. (p.54)

## APPENDIX B

# Historical Footnotes
[compiled for your convenience by the
staff of the *Coming Home Network*]

1  Pope Gregory VII, in his 1075 *Dictatus Papae* ("Dictates of the Pope"), demanded for the pope a type of supremacy never claimed by his predecessors, including the right to use imperial insignia, to depose emperors, and to release subjects from their oath of allegiance to unjust rulers. On the other side, the imperialists asserted the right of the emperor to intervene in the appointment of bishops and in the affairs of the papacy. They also claimed that the emperor had the right to control the election of the pope and to depose him if he was unworthy. As a result the emperor would become the ultimate arbiter in the government of the Church. Neither of these extreme views—papal or imperialist—was representative of the common opinion of the time. (p.11)

2  Refers to the tension at the time between the secular and the holy, hence 'regnum' (rule) and 'sacerdotium' (sacred). (p.11)

3  Investiture at this period meant that on the death of a bishop or abbot, the king was accustomed to select a successor and to bestow on him the ring and staff with the words: *Accipe ecclesiam* (accept this church). (p.11)

4  The Hohenstaufens were consistent opponents of both papal authority and Italian independence. Conrad Hohenstaufen was the nephew of Henry V. He was excommunicated with all his followers, among whom was the archbishop of Milan. Conrad became the first Hohenstaufen emperor (1138-1152). (p.11)

5  A *bulla* was originally a circular plate or boss of metal, so called from its resemblance in form to a bubble floating upon water (Lat. *bullire*, to boil). In the course of time the term came to be applied to the leaden seals with which papal and royal documents were authenticated in the early Middle Ages, and by a further development, the name, from designating the seal, was eventually attached to the document itself. (p.11)

6  A letter addressed December 5, 1301 by Pope Boniface V
   Philip the Fair, King of France. Philip was at enmity with the
   Under the pretext of his royal rights, Philip conferred benefices,
   appointed bishops to sees, regardless of papal authority. He dro
   from their sees those bishops who, in opposition to his w
   remained faithful to the Pope. This letter is couched in firm b
   paternal terms. It points out the evils the king has brought to h
   kingdom, to Church, and State; and invites him to do penance an
   mend his ways. It was unheeded by the king, and was followed by
   the famous Bull *Unam Sanctam.* (p.11)

7  Spiritual Franciscans felt that St. Francis's *Testament* (prescribing
   poverty and the reliance on alms-giving for the Franciscan Order) was
   to be taken literally. After Francis' death, the rules on poverty were
   relaxed so that the Franciscans could possess material goods. The
   Spiritual Franciscans were vehemently opposed to this modification,
   and continued to criticize both the Order and the papacy. The movement was founded by Joachim of Fiore (1132-1202), a contemporary
   of St. Francis, and later condemned as a heretical sect. (p.12)

8  The name used for the legislature of the German empire, or Holy
   Roman Empire, from the 12th century to 1806. (p.12)

9  Latin. *ex*, out of, and *communio* or *communicatio*, communion–
   exclusion from the communion. The severest censure is a medicinal,
   spiritual penalty that deprives the culpable Christian of all partic-
   ipation in the common blessings of ecclesiastical society. Being a
   penalty, it supposes culpability; and being the most serious penalty
   that the Church can impose, it naturally supposes a very grave
   offense. The penalty is "medicinal" rather than "vindictive," the
   intention being not to punish but to correct the Christian and bring
   him back to the path of righteousness. (p.12)

10 A censure forbidding the faithful, while still remaining in communion
   with the Church, the use of certain sacred privileges, such as
   Christian burial, some of the sacraments, and attendance at litur-
   gical services. It does not exclude from Church membership, nor
   does it necessarily imply a personal fault of any individual affected
   by the interdict. When imposed for a fixed period, it is a significant
   penalty because of some grave act done against the common good
   of the Church by one or more parishes. Usual religious services are
   curtailed, but sacraments may be given to the dying, marriages celebrated, and Holy Communion administered if the interdict is

general or local (not personal). A general interdict may be imposed only by the Holy See. Parishes or persons may be interdicted only by the local ordinary. (p.12)

[11] Etym. Latin *vicarius*, substituting, acting for; from *vicis*, change, turn, office. Being the visible head of Christ's Church on earth, acting for and in the place of Christ, the pope possesses supreme authority in the Catholic Church. The title "Vicar of Christ" was applied to the pope from at least the eighth century and gradually replaced the former title, "Vicar of St. Peter." Its biblical basis is Christ's commission of Peter to "feed my lambs, feed my sheep" (John 21:15-17), thus making him His Vicar and fulfilling the promise made in Matthew 16:18-19. (p.12)

[12] *Defensor pacis* ("Defender of the peace"), published in 1517, is divided into three books: the first deals with a philosophy of the state, the second with the theology of the church, and the third is a summary. The author, Marsilius, argued that the unifying element in society is the state and not the church. In book two he chastised the papacy for causing dissension in the world as it attempted to control the temporal world. He believed Christ supported submission to temporal power and that any papal claims for control were invalid. He believed the general council was supreme over the pope in the Church. (p.12)

[13] Pope Clement V came to Avignon in 1309, where he was received by the Dominicans. He had no intention of establishing himself permanently, nor of creating a new Christian capital in Avignon. It was, nonetheless, the role that the city would play for about seventy years, including six other Popes after Clement V. Rome, in the early 1300s, was torn by rival clans, prey to constant riots and uprisings. After the schism between the Eastern and Western Church, Rome found herself outside the center of Catholic Christianity, of which the kingdoms of France and England formed the two great rival powers. Living in France gave the Pope a more comfortable and centrally located home from which to rule. St. Catherine of Sienna was instrumental in moving the papal residences back to Rome in 1377. The choice of Avignon as a permanent residence was essentially the result of political considerations. (p.12)

[14] The financial arm of the papal administration. (p.12)

[15] Strictly speaking, the ensemble of departments or ministries which assist the pope in the government of the Universal Church. (p.13)

[16] A papal court assigned all contentious cases that required a judicial investigation with proof. (p.14)

[17] The Western Schism consisted of two rival claimants for the papacy, each with his own court, one in Rome and one in Avignon; and before long a third claimant in Pisa. After the death of Pope Gregory XI, the Roman people demanded the election of a Roman; and the cardinals chose the Archbishop of Bari, who took the name of Urban VI. He immediately began to attack the immorality and worldliness of the clergy, and therein created many enemies. He also alienated a number of his supporters by several hasty and arbitrary acts, and by public rebukes to prelates and cardinals—despite the warnings of St. Catherine of Siena, who begged him to be more tactful. After he had declared his purpose of creating a majority of Italian cardinals and of never transferring the papal residence back to France, thirteen cardinals, encouraged by the French king, Charles V, announced in 1378 that Pope Urban's election had been invalid, and chose Cardinal Robert of Geneva to be Pope. Robert took the name of Clement VII, and the Great Schism of the West had begun. Pope Boniface IX (1389-1404) succeeded Pope Urban VI. Failing to secure Church unity by winning over the Avignon Pope, Clement VII, he excommunicated him. The Schism lasted until Pope Martin V's election in 1417. (p.14)

[18] Ultramontani were those who were part of a movement that wanted to terminate the power over the Church of Enlightenment rationalism, especially as this was realized in the secularist state domination of the Church since Louis XIV's time. Structurally, Utramontanism meant centralization of the Church under papal authority, coupled by independence of the Church from state control. (p.14)

[19] A council may fail to secure the approbation of the whole Church or of the Pope, and thus not rank in authority with Ecumenical councils. Such was the case with the Robber Synod of 449 (*Latrocinium Ephesinum*), the Synod of Pisa in 1409, and in part with the Councils of Constance and Basle. (p.15)

[20] A (partly) ecumenical council held at Constance, now in the Grand Duchy of Baden, from Nov. 5, 1414 to April 22, 1418. This secured the withdrawal or deposition of the three rival popes, and had supplied a strong argument in favor of the conciliar theory (supremacy of councils over the pope). It is clear both from the speeches of some of the Fathers of Constance as well as from its decrees that such a

feeling was rapidly gaining ground, and that many people had come to regard the government of the Church by general councils, convoked at regular intervals, as the one most in harmony with the needs of the time. (p.15)

21 Favoritism shown to "nephews" in appointments to desirable positions. (p.16)

22 Pope Innocent VIII's Bull against witches must be understood in its historical context. In that age belief in the existence of witches and in the possibility of communicating with the powers of darkness prevailed among the people. The witch craze and witch burnings were not limited to a single religion, or to any one nationality, or to Europe. The mixed clerical-secular criminal trials manifest themselves rather as phenomena typical of that age in the general history of law. Unfortunately, Innocent's Bull drew attention to the particular practices attributed to witches, and it did help to spread belief in the alleged phenomena, but there was no intention of committing the Church to a belief in witchcraft. (p.16)

23 St. Catherine of Siena, Dominican Tertiary, born 1347, died 1380; St. Catherine of Bolgna, Poor Clare and mystical writer, born 1413, died 1463; St. Catherine of Genoa, Born in 1447, died 1510. (p.17)

24 An anonymous treatise that emphasized humility, self-negation, and a mystical union with God. The work impressed Martin Luther, who thought he found in it precedents for his own theology, and he published a complete edition in 1518 with a preface in which he stated: "no book except the Bible and St. Augustine has come to my attention from which I have learned more about God, Christ, man and all things." The book does not, however, teach Luther's theology. (p.17)

25 *Devotio moderna* or "new devotion" was a movement of men and women begun by Gerard Groote. Most historians have seen the movement as a reaction to the ecclesiastical and secular problems that dominated the times. (p.17)

26 *The Angelus* is a short practice of devotion in honor of the Incarnation of our Lord repeated three times each day, morning, noon, and evening, at the sound of a bell. From the first word of the three versicles, i.e. *Angelus Domini nuntiavit Mariae* (The angel of the Lord declared unto Mary), the devotion derives its name. (p.18)

27 Also called *Stations of the Cross*, *Via Crucis*, and *Via Dolorosa*. These names are used to signify either a series of pictures or tableaux

representing certain scenes in the Passion of Christ, each corresponding to a particular incident, or the special form of devotion connected with such representations. (p.18)

28 Extreme Unction was a term used for centuries for the Sacrament of the anointing of the sick. It is 'unction' because a person is anointed with oil; it is 'extreme' because it is conferred on those who are considered *in extremis*, i.e., in extreme physical disability with the likelihood of dying. (p.19)

29 In the language of religious men and women, the world (*saeculum*) is opposed to the cloister; religious who follow a rule, especially those who have been ordained, form the regular clergy, while those who live in the world are called the secular clergy. (p.20)

30 Mendicant Friars are members of those religious orders which, originally, by vow of poverty renounced all proprietorship not only individually but also (and in this differing from the monks) in common, relying for support on their own work and on the charity of the faithful. Hence the name of "begging friars." (p.20)

31 The Béguines were members of sisterhoods founded in the Netherlands in the 12th century. Without common rule or hierarchy, free to hold private property, they were allowed to leave the sisterhood to marry. They emphasized and supported themselves by manual labor or by teaching. Beghards were their mail counterparts, who held no private property and had a common fund. (p.31)

32 By Communion is meant the actual reception of the Sacrament of the Eucharist. (p.22)

33 The word *relics* comes from the Latin *reliquiae* (the counterpart of the Greek *leipsana*) which already before the propagation of Christianity was used in its modern sense, viz., of some object, notably part of the body or clothes, remaining as a memorial of a departed saint. (p.22)

34 The word *indulgence* (Lat. *indulgentia*, from *indulgeo*, to be kind or tender) originally meant kindness or favor; in post-classic Latin it came to mean the remission of a tax or debt. In Roman law and in the Vulgate of the Old Testament it was used to express release from captivity or punishment. In theological language the word is sometimes employed in its primary sense to signify the kindness and mercy of God. But in the special sense in which it is here considered, an indulgence is a remission of the temporal punishment due to sin, the guilt of which has already been forgiven. (p.22)

35 A legate is one whom the pope sends to sovereigns, governments or to the members of the episcopate and faithful of a country, as his representative, to treat of Church matters or even on a mission of honor. (p.23)

36 A fanatical and heretical sect that flourished in the thirteenth and succeeding centuries. Followers were often accustomed to beating themselves in public processions as an act of penance. (p.24)

37 By this term is usually meant a special ecclesiastical institution for combating or suppressing heresy. (p.25)

38 The essential characteristic of the Catharist faith was Dualism, i.e. the belief in a good and an evil principle, of whom the former created the invisible and spiritual universe, while the latter was the author of the material world. (p.25)

39 "There is nothing more serious than the sacrilege of schism because there is no just cause for severing [the] unity [of the Church" (*Contra epistolam Parmeniani*, lib. II, cap. XI, in Migne, *Patrologia Latina*, vol. 43, col. 69). (p.26)

40 Cardinals are appointed by the pope to assist and advise him in the government of the Church. It is they who elect the next pope. (p.28)

41 Based on the scholastic theologian, John Duns Scotus (1266-1308). Scotus argued that faith was a matter of will and could not be supported by logical proofs. This division between philosophy and faith was to have far-reaching effects. Although arguing for the existence of God from efficiency, finality, and the degrees of perfection, he taught that all other knowledge of the divine, including the Resurrection and immortality, must be accepted by sheer belief. Creation, he believed, was the effect of God's love as He extends His goodness to creatures so that they will love Him freely. Grace, then, is identical with love and has its origin in the will. Because of his idea of the superiority of the will over the intellect, Duns Scotus believed that heaven consists of sharing the love of God. Divine love can best be seen in Jesus Christ who would have come, Scotus taught, even if man had not sinned. Thus the Incarnation as the center and end of the universe was not determined by original sin. Scholars in the Franciscan school ("Scotists" who followed him) moved ever further in the separation of faith and reason, leading to the eventual decline of Scholasticism. (p.32)

42 Metaphysics is the science of being, as being; or of the absolutely first principles of being. It is also called ontology, first philosophy,

the philosophy of being, or the philosophy of first causes. (p.32)

43 Scholasticism is the system of philosophy and theology first developed in the medieval schools of Christian Europe, having a scholastic or technical language and methodology. It was built on the writings of the Church Fathers, notably St. Augustine, using many of the philosophical principles and insights of Aristotle and Neoplatonism. It was co-ordinated into a synthesis of human and divine wisdom by St. Thomas Aquinas. (p.32)

44 Contrary to the official teaching of the Catholic Church (as expounded by St. Thomas Aquinas), William of Ockham taught that reality could not give evidence or provide scientific support for God's existence. He criticized the accommodation of the philosophical system of Aristotle with Christian doctrine that had been fashioned by Aquinas, who achieved an accord between faith and reason. Ockham rejected this teaching on the basis of a radical empiricism in which the basis of knowledge is direct experience of individual things (ontological nominalism). According to Ockham, universals are created by reason, essences have no independent reality of their own, but are only names or mere vocal utterances. Reality was a collection of absolute singulars and, therefore, could not give evidence or provide scientific support for God's existence. God to Ockham was above all knowledge, and thus could not be apprehended by reason, as the Thomists taught, or by illumination, as the Augustinians believed, but only by faith. (p.32)

45 The Catholic view of God is that God acts intelligently. His choice accords with his own nature and wisdom, and so is not arbitrary. While God is not required to create, if he creates, it is impossible for him to contradict himself. Since natures reflect his wisdom, God could not, for example, create a triangle that does not have three sides because it would be contradictory. God could not create a human being and not orient him to what is truly the perfection of a human being. And God could not damn someone who had not refused him not because God's power is limited, but because to do so would contradict his own wisdom and love. Luther had the idea that the relation between morality and religion was such that morality (since it goes back to God's arbitrary will) is something that can be left behind, like leaving the foothills when climbing the mountain (of God). But the Catholic understanding is that morality can never be left behind, because God is (by nature) good. (p.32)

[46] The term "Pre-Lutheran Thomism" refers to the scholastic philosophy of St. Thomas Aquinas, as explained in footnote n.44. On the surface, Ockham's and Luther's doctrine of justification may not appear to be significantly different than the Catholic Church's teaching. However, the differences are both important and considerable. According to the Catholic Church, God's love is primary but his love interiorly transforms the person, mysteriously introducing the divine life into the soul of the human person. Although human nature has been wounded, it has not been totally corrupted. Our cooperation with God's grace is therefore necessary and effective in the process of becoming justified. God declares us just because we truly have been made, through God's grace, just. According to Luther, the justification of the person is not a process of becoming a righteous person and, therefore, one who is justified. It is a one time declarative act on God's part due to a mere external imputation of Christ's righteousness (i.e., because of Christ's merits on Calvary God acts *as if* we are transformed although we really have not been). According to Luther we are simply "declared" or "recognized" by God to be just. Our sins are "covered" rather than eradicated. (p.33)

[47] Semi-pelagianism was a spurious doctrine of grace advocated by monks of Southern Gaul at and around Marseilles after 428. It aimed at a compromise between the two extremes of Pelagianism and Augustinism, and was condemned as heresy at the Ecumenical Council of Orange in 529 after disputes extending over more than a hundred years. (p.34)

[48] Lat. *Scrupulus*, "a small sharp, or pointed, stone," hence, in a transferred sense, "uneasiness of mind." An unfounded apprehension and consequently unwarranted fear that something is a sin which, as a matter of fact, is not. It is not considered here so much as an isolated act, but rather as an habitual state of mind known to directors of souls as "a scrupulous conscience." (p.34)

[49] The most widely accepted specifically Lutheran Confession, or statement of faith. It was prepared by the German religious reformer Melanchthon, Martin Luther's collaborator and friend, as a summary document for the German nobility, who were called to a Diet at Augsburg in 1530, by the Holy Roman emperor Charles V to present their Lutheran views. Rejected there and later amended, the Confession—together with the Nicene, Apostles', and

Athanasian creeds and Luther's Small Catechism and Large Catechism—constitutes the creedal basis for Lutherans. (p.40)

50 19th Ecumenical Council (for the whole Church, not just a single geographic area); opened December 13, 1545, and closed on December 4, 1563. Its main object was the definitive determination of the doctrines of the Church in answer to the teachings of the Protestants. (p.46)

51 20th Ecumenical Council; opened December 8, 1869 and closed on July 18, 1870. (p.46)

52 Etym. Latin, *regula*, a rule; norm; measure. The difference between "rule of faith" and "rule of discipline" is significant, and often the two are confused in Protestant circles. The rule of faith is the teaching of the Church based on divine revelation (the Word of God in Sacred Scripture and Sacred Tradition), and therefore it is the norm that enables the Christian to know what to believe. For example, the Trinity is a rule of faith. The rule of discipline is a customary standard that has been put into place by the Church to govern its members in its various forms of worship and the general living of the Christian life. As such, disciplines can be altered by the Church, such as the discipline of celibacy, rules on fasting, etc. (p.49)

53 A heresy of the fifth century, named after Pelagius, a Christian moralist, which denied original sin as well as Christian grace. (p.50)

54 Based on the theology of St. Thomas Aquinas (1227-1274). (p.52)

55 This Disputation occurred between Luther and Karlstadt on one side and Eck on the other and lasted from June 27 until July 15, 1519. Both sides claimed the victory. (p.57)

56 'Lift up your heart!'; one of the admonitions of the priest to the congregants in the Mass. (p.58)

57 An ordinary and permanent representative of the pope. (p.59)

58 The chair or throne or See of Peter, referring to the office of the papacy. (p.61)

59 Convoked by Pope Martin V in 1431, closed at Lausanne in 1449. It succeeded in fixing the eyes of the world upon the abuses, but without the pope it lacked sufficient authority to carry through the necessary reforms. As a consequence the secular rulers undertook what the ecclesiastical authority had failed to set right. It struck a terrible blow at the rights of the Holy See and shook men's faith in the pope's spiritual power at a time when his temporal sovereignty was in imminent danger. (p.62)

[60] Followers of Philip Melancthon, Luther's collaborator and friend, were called Philippists or Crypto-Calvinists. About fourteen years after his death, largely due to persecution, they began to adopt more and more of the Calvinist ideology and reject the Lutheran tenants, even on the issue of predestination. (p.62)

[61] Pietism was a movement within the ranks of Protestantism, originating in the reaction against fruitless Protestant orthodoxy of the seventeenth century, and aiming at the revival of devotion and practical Christianity. Its appearance in the German Lutheran Church, about 1670, is connected with Philipp Jakob Spener, a German Lutheran Pietist leader. Spener was raised in a highly protective and deeply religious atmosphere characterized by a mixture of Puritanism and Arndtian Pietistic mysticism. He proclaimed the necessity of conversion and holy living. As Spener's popularity spread, he became an increasingly controversial figure and his disciples were even expelled from Leipzig in 1690. (p.62)

[62] As of 1981, 20,800 Christian Protestant denominations were listed in the Oxford University Press's World Christian Encyclopedia. The disintegration of Protestantism into so many competing factions, teaching different doctrines on key theological issues only further affirms Adam's point made nearly fifty years ago. (p.62)

[63] From Gnosticism, the theory of salvation by knowledge. Gnostics claimed to know the mysteries of the universe. They borrowed what suited their purpose from the Gospels, wrote new gospels of their own, and in general proposed a dualistic system of belief. Gnosticism is the invariable element in every major Christian heresy, by its denial of an objective revelation that was completed in the apostolic age and its disclaimer that Christ established in the Church a teaching authority to interpret decisively the meaning of the revealed word of God. (p.66)

[64] Statement prepared in 1537 by Martin Luther and his followers of "articles of our doctrine [in order that it might be plain] in case of deliberation as to what and how far we would be both willing and able to yield to the Papists, and in what points we intended to persevere and abide to the end." (from the Introduction to the Articles) (p.67)

[65] For those outside the Catholic Church, this is undoubtedly one of the most difficult paragraphs in the book. On the surface it may sound inexcusably arrogant or uncharitable, especially in our age of

"ecumenism." However, given how the Catholic Church understands her mission and identity, we hope the reader will at least understand that the Catholic Church can accept nothing less than her responsibility through Christ as the one means of salvation. "Guarding the Deposit of Faith is the mission which the Lord entrusted to His Church, and which she fulfills in every age" (Pope John Paul II, *Catechism of the Catholic Church*, page 1). For further explanation of the Catholic Church's teaching on *Extra Ecclesiam nulla salus* (no salvation outside the Church), please see the *Catechism of the Catholic Church* nn. 813ff—Editor. (p.73)

## Appendix C
# Further Reading Materials

Adam, Karl. *Spirit of Catholicism* (Steubenville: Franciscan University Press, 1996). A classic study of the essence of Catholicism that is well worth reading.

Belloc, Hilaire. *How the Reformation Happened* (Rockford: TAN Books and Publishers, Inc., 1992). A very enjoyable and eye-opening presentation of a Catholic perspective on the English Reformation.

Belloc, Hilaire. *Characters of the Reformation* (Rockford: TAN Books and Publishers, Inc., 1992). An excellent book presenting a portrait of the principal people involved in the Reformation.

Daniel-Rops, Henri. *The Protestant Reformation*, 2 vols. (New York: Image Books, 1963). A classic retelling of all the issues, people and events of the Reformation period.

Daniel-Rops, Henri. *The Catholic Reformation*, 2 vols. (New York: Image Books, 1963).

Cobbett, William. *A History of the Protestant Reformation in England and Ireland* (Rockford: TAN Books and Publishers, Inc., 1988). Originally written between 1824 and 1827 by an English Protestant, this book has been reprinted many times because it presents the often untold story of the Reformation in England during the 16th century. Cobbett shows how the Reformers were not only successful in eradicating the Catholic Faith from their land, but he looks at the consequences that befell the country as a result.

Hahn, Scott and Kimberly. *Rome Sweet Home* (San Francisco: Ignatius Press, 1993). One of the most well publicized conversion stories in the late twentieth century.

Grodi, Marcus, ed. *Journeys Home* (Santa Barabara: Queenship Publishing, 1997). The conversion stories of Protestant clergy and laity entering the Catholic Church.

Howell, Kenneth. *Mary of Nazareth* (Santa Barbara: Queenship Publishing, 1998). Howell explores Scripture to show that by knowing Mary better, we come to know better Jesus her Son.

Keys, Paul. 95 *Reasons To Become A Catholic* (Steubenville: The Coming Home Network, 1998). A former Presbyterian pastor briefly and clearly enumerates the 95 reasons that compelled him to enter the Catholic Church.

Shea, Mark. *By What Authority? An Evangelical Discovers Catholic Tradition* (Huntington: Our Sunday Visitor, 1996). Interspersed with his own journey from evangelicalism to the Catholic Church, Shea skillfully explains how and why Sacred Tradition occupies a central role in divine Revelation.

Keating, Karl. *Catholicism and Fundamentalism* (San Francisco: Ignatius Press, 1988). This book, which effectively refutes the common fundamentalist misconceptions of and attacks on the Catholic Church, has served as the initial stepping stone for many modern converts.

Sungenis, Robert. *Not By Faith Alone* (Santa Barbara: Queenship Publishing, 1997). A biblical study of the Catholic doctrine of Justification.

Sungenis, Robert. *Not By Scripture Alone* (Santa Barbara: Queenship Publishing, 1999). A Catholic critique of the Protestant doctrine of *sola scriptura*.

For other excellent resources, please visit the *CHNetwork* web site at www.chnetwork.org

## APPENDIX D

# What is *The Coming Home Network*?

The *Coming Home Network* (*CHNetwork*) began in 1993 out of the seemingly isolated experiences of several Protestant clergy and their spouses. Upon leaving their pastorates to enter the Catholic Church, these clergy and their families discovered with surprise that there were many others being drawn by the Spirit to take the same journey "home."

Although this is not generally known, Protestant clergy and laity from across the denominational spectrum are entering the Catholic Church. They come with great enthusiasm and commitment to follow Jesus Christ wherever He leads, even if this means coming out of their previously comfortable and familiar spiritual surroundings.

Now, every week the Lord adds new names to the *CHNetwork* membership as clergy and laity from other traditions seek assistance and encouragement as they contemplate the possibility of entering the Catholic Church.

The *CHNetwork* has been featured in many national publications, and on the EWTN television network where the *CHNetwork's* founder and president, Marcus Grodi, hosts a weekly live television program entitled *The Journey Home*.

The *CHNetwork* helps inquiring clergy as well as laity of other traditions on their journey by providing contacts, assistance, fellowship, email-based communication, web site information, regional retreats, a network of volunteer helpers, literature such as the *Coming Home Journal* and many other helpful resources.

## How can I Become a Member?

If you are interested in becoming a member of the *CHNetwork* please write, email or call us. A $25 annual donation is greatly appreciated to cover the costs of printing and mailing the newsletter, the Journal, our other resources such as this book by Karl Adam, as well as other administrative and apostolic expenses.

*The Coming Home Network International*
P.O. Box 4100
Steubenville, OH  43952
800-664-5110
info@chnetwork.org
www.chnetwork.org